The Fac_ __
Bible John

The unsolved Barrowland Ballroom murders and the search for a Scottish serial killer

Murder World

Scotland

Book 5

Murder World: Real crimes, real killers.

Table of Contents

Introduction

It was seven o'clock on a February Friday morning when Morris Goodman left his house on Carmichael Place in the Queen's Park area of Glasgow. It was getting light, though the sun wouldn't rise for another half hour and it was bitterly cold. A few stars were still visible in the clear sky and Morris pushed his hands deep into the pockets of his heavy work jacket and hunched his shoulders against the cold as his boots crunched on a thick layer of frost. His breath plumed in front of him like steam as he walked towards the lane where he kept his car in a lock-up garage. Good thing too, he thought, otherwise he'd have to spend another five minutes fumbling in the cold, scraping the ice off a frozen windscreen.

At sixty-seven, Morris felt the cold more than he had as a young man. By rights, he should really have been retired by now, but he still enjoyed his work as a cabinet maker. He turned into the narrow, cobbled, high-walled lane and the cold seemed even more intense. Morris' eyesight wasn't quite what it had been in his younger days either, and there were no street lights in the lane. When he saw something on the ramp outside his lock-up at the far end, he squinted to make out what it was in the half-light. His first thought was that it was a shop-window dummy lying on the ground.

Then he wondered whether it might be some unfortunate vagrant who was spending the night sleeping in the open?

As he got closer, he realised to his growing horror that he was looking at a naked woman, lying on her back on the frosty ground. Just for a fleeting moment he thought that she might be asleep. Then, he saw the livid marks on her neck. Closer still he saw that frost had filmed over her open and unblinking eyes which were looking sightlessly towards the lightening sky. Carefully, he crouched and touched her shoulder. It was icy and hard. Gasping for breath, Morris stumbled back towards his house and the telephone.

That was how it began.

***

Just like any other country, Scotland has its share of unsolved crimes. However, few have proved to be as enduring as the story of the man who killed three women in Glasgow in the late 1960s and became known as Bible John.

This murderer picked up each of his three victims at the Barrowland Ballroom in the east of the city centre. The bodies of all three women were later found dumped. All three were mothers, all had been menstruating at the time of their death and all were beaten and strangled. In each case, the women's handbags had been removed from the crime scene.

The murderer made no attempt to conceal or disguise himself and was seen by a number of witnesses with his victims at the ballroom and outside - one witness actually shared a taxi with the killer and one of his victims. Through discussions with these witnesses, a well-known artist working on behalf of the police produced a striking portrait of a man with red hair and blue/grey eyes and wearing a cold, rather supercilious expression. This portrait was widely publicized and became known as the face of Bible John. People wondered how the man could possibly avoid arrest with his likeness on the front of every major Scottish newspaper and on police posters throughout Glasgow? What was less well known was that, while some witnesses agreed that the portrait did look like the killer, others were equally certain that it didn't resemble him at all.

Despite all the publicity and a massive police investigation, Bible John was never caught.

In the years since there have been a number of attempts to provide an identity for Bible John, some using new technology such as DNA analysis. On several occasions it has seemed that we were on the brink of finally knowing who this killer was, but in each case this has proved to be a vain hope. These later efforts have certainly revealed some new suspects but, to date, the killer has still not been positively identified.

How can this be possible? The murderer frequented a busy public place and was seen with his victims by a number of witnesses who got a good look at him. By the time of the third murder, there had been massive publicity and people were on their guard and actually looking for a potential killer. Given that, just how did this person manage to kill three times and yet still escape detection? Having killed three times, why did he stop? Did he really stop at all or did he just become more adept at hiding his crimes? Did Bible John actually really exist at all?

This book provides details of the murders themselves, the police investigation in 1968/1969 and subsequent investigations and theories. It looks at the suspects who have been identified as Bible John over the years and assesses the likelihood of any of these suspects being the killer.

Almost fifty years on, it seems that there is still new information waiting to be pieced together in the search for Scotland's most elusive serial killer.

Prologue

The Barras, to the east of the city centre in Glasgow, is a special place. During the Victorian period, changes in farming practice and a reducing need for farm labourers brought an influx of people to the cities of Scotland, both from the Highlands and from Ireland. The city of Glasgow was no exception and the vast majority of the incomers seeking a new life in the city were cripplingly poor.

At that time, there was no open-air market in Glasgow where those with little money could make a few pennies by selling second-hand goods to those even poorer than themselves. In the mid-1800s an impromptu market began to develop in the Bridgegate area of the city, where there were already several rag and bone merchants. The new traders arrived with handcarts from which they sold their wares. These carts were known in the local vernacular as *'barras'* (barrows) and the area where they congregated quickly became known as the *'barralands'* or simply the *'barra*s.'

Initially, the Barras market was mainly used for the sale of second-hand clothes, gathered by hawkers from the more affluent areas of the city. Later it expanded into a flea-market and a place where stolen goods were openly bought and sold. By the beginning of the twentieth century, it had become the largest open-air market in Europe.

At around that time an astute Glaswegian Woman named Maggie McIvor realized the commercial potential in this area and she and her husband began to buy up property and to lease out sales pitches and barrows. The McIvors also began to formalize the market by placing some stalls within a covered area. By 1931 the market was completely enclosed and Maggie (by this time known to one and all as the *Barras Queen*) decided to have a ballroom built on the first floor above the market stalls. Partly this was done to ensure that Maggie would have a place to hold her annual Christmas dance, but also because she recognized the business potential in a ballroom.

The original Barrowland Ballroom

The dance hall was opened in 1934 as the Barrowland

Ballroom and, with resident band Billy McGregor and the Gaybirds, it became one of the most popular dance venues in Glasgow. By the time that American servicemen arrived during World War Two, bringing with them such new dances as the jitterbug and the jive, weekend queues regularly reached round the block.

Then, in June 1958, Maggie McIvor (who was by this time a millionaire) died and, just three months later, the market and dance hall she had created were destroyed in a fire. Maggie's family re-built the dance hall and the new Barrowland Ballroom was opened on Christmas Eve 1960. The new dance floor was a wonder – made from thousands of pieces of specially imported Canadian Maple laid in a criss-cross pattern, it was given extra spring by being laid over thousands of tennis balls, each cut in half.

The timing for the opening of the new venue was immaculate. By the late 1950s, dance halls were the UK's second most popular form of entertainment (behind the cinema) with over two hundred million customers each year (at a time when the combined attendance at football matches across the UK was less than eighty million per year). A newspaper survey at the time suggested that as many as 70% of all married couples in the UK had first met at a dance hall.

In Glasgow, dance halls were even more popular than in other parts of the UK. By 1960, the city had fourteen permanent dance halls and the Locarno, the Majestic and the Plaza were some of the largest and most luxurious in the country.

However, just when it seemed that dance halls were here to stay, suddenly and inexplicably, they began to decline. Some people have blamed the introduction of television which was persuading people to spend evenings in their own homes. Others have suggested that increasing mixing of the sexes in the workplace and other social settings meant that dance halls were no longer necessary as a place to meet a potential boy or girlfriend. Whatever the reason, by the end of the 1960s, very few dance halls were still in business. A few had transformed themselves into more trendy discos and some had become bingo halls but the majority had closed down.

One of the few that survived in Glasgow was the Barrowland Ballroom. Even by the late 1960s this was still a popular place for young people to congregate at weekends. Then, one evening in February 1968, something happened at the Barrowland Ballroom that would lead to it being remembered for something very different to dancing, flirting and music...

Part 1: The Murders

'I'm sorry son, your wife's been murdered.'

Joe Beattie

Chapter 1: Patricia Docker

Twenty-five year old Patricia Docker loved dancing. That's how she had met her husband Alex. But now she and Alex were separated. Her husband was still a Corporal in the RAF and serving at RAF Digby in Lincolnshire. Patricia had come back to Glasgow, her home town, with her four year old son Alex and moved back in with her parents in their house at 29, Langside Place near Queens Park. Between looking after a lively toddler and working as an Auxiliary Nurse at Mearnskirk Hospital in Renfrewshire, there wasn't much time to dance, so Patricia was delighted when it was agreed that her parents would look after young Alex on Thursday 22nd February 1968 while she went out dancing with friends from the hospital.

Patricia was an attractive woman. Just five feet and three inches tall, she was a slim brunette with a cheeky smile and a pair of gentle hazel eyes. She left her parents house on Langside Place that Thursday evening and headed off to meet her friends at the Majestic Ballroom on Hope Street in the centre of Glasgow and on the other side of the River Clyde. She had her wavy hair cut in a fashionable bob and she was wearing a yellow, knitted dress under her heavy duffel coat – February evenings in Glasgow can be cold!

Patricia arrived at the Majestic Ballroom (known locally as the '*Magic Stick*') where she met her friends. They listened to the resident band, Dr. Crock and his Crackpots, who performed favourites including 'Yellow River' and 'Butterfingers' and a version of a new hit by Marmalade, 'Obladi, Oblada.' But, at some point later in the evening Patricia seems to have decided to move on to the Barrowland Ballroom without her friends. The Majestic closed at ten-thirty on a Thursday evening so it's possible that Patricia may have simply wanted more dancing (the Barrowland Ballroom didn't close until midnight). She may also have been attracted by the knowledge that Thursday and Saturday nights at the Barrowlands were '*Palais Nights*' when, from 8pm to midnight, only over-25s were admitted (these were generally locally referred to as '*Grab-a-Granny*' nights).

These over-25 nights at the Barrowland Ballroom had a certain reputation. These were where married men and women in search of a little uncomplicated companionship were said to congregate. There were standing jokes about attendees at these nights pausing as they entered to remove wedding rings. One retired Glasgow police officer memorably referred to the ballroom as '*Sodom and Gomorrah.*' A Glasgow resident who had spent time at the ballroom remembered: '*It was well known that if you wanted a bit more than a dance, then Thursday night was the evening to visit the Barrowland. I don't think many used their actual name on a Thursday night, folk were cautious, anything that happened after dancing was finished was usually a one-off.'* Perhaps Patricia always intended to go to the Barrowland Ballroom that night, but told her parents that she was going to the decidedly more respectable Majestic so that they wouldn't worry about her?

Whatever her reasons, Patricia went to the Barrowland Ballroom without any of her friends from the hospital. Several people remembered seeing her in her distinctive yellow dress, dancing with a number of partners, and more than one witness later recalled seeing her dancing with a red-haired man, but no-one noticed when she left or whether she was alone. That evening, the dancing stopped at around 11:30pm, as it always did, and by midnight the ballroom was empty.

***

Around seven o'clock the following morning, Friday 23rd February, sixty-seven year old joiner Morris Goodman was on his way to work when he entered a lane close to Carmichael Place where he kept his car in a lock-up garage. The lane was less than four hundred meters from the house on Langside Place where Patricia Docker's four year old son lay sleeping. It was bitterly cold and there was a heavy frost on the ground. Goodman saw something lying in the lane – at first thought he was looking at a drunk or a vagrant sleeping it off. As he got closer, to his horror he realized that he was looking at the naked body of a young woman. He immediately returned to his house and called the police.

The police on the scene were two traffic officers who happened to be in the area. By eight o'clock the first detectives had arrived, Detective Sergeant Andrew Johnstone and Detective Constable Norman MacDonald. They began their investigation and it was clear from the outset that this was murder. The woman was lying on her back and was naked other than for one shoe. She had been badly beaten on the face and head and the livid bruises on her neck made it clear that she had been strangled. There was no sign of clothing or a handbag and no way of establishing the victim's identity. Dr. James Imrie, the police pathologist, arrived not long after the first detectives. He noticed that rigor mortis was well established, confirming that the woman had been dead for several hours.

A door-to-door enquiry by uniformed police was started within two hours of the discovery of the body but it failed to produce any really useful information. One woman living in the area claimed that she had heard a woman cry out *'leave me alone!'* twice, in the early hours and another thought that she might have seen someone answering the victim's description getting into a car in the vicinity, but neither account could be definitely tied-in to the body in the lane.

A journalist was found who had been hosting a party the night before in the immediate area. There had been a large number of guests and people had been arriving and leaving until the early hours, but no-one had seen anything odd. John Wilson, Patricia Docker's father, read an account of the discovery of the still unidentified body in the evening paper, but he didn't immediately associate it with Patricia. The Wilson's were only mildly concerned that Patricia hadn't come home after her evening of dancing and they both assumed that she had gone to stay at the house of a friend, something she had done before.

It wasn't until an ambulance driver saw the body at the morgue at Victoria Hospital where it had been taken that there was any clue as to who the dead woman was. Despite her facial injuries, the driver believed that he knew her and that she was a nurse. This was confirmed when John Wilson arrived the following day at a police station with a photograph of Patricia and told police that his daughter hadn't come home. He was taken to the morgue where he identified the body of the dead woman as his daughter.

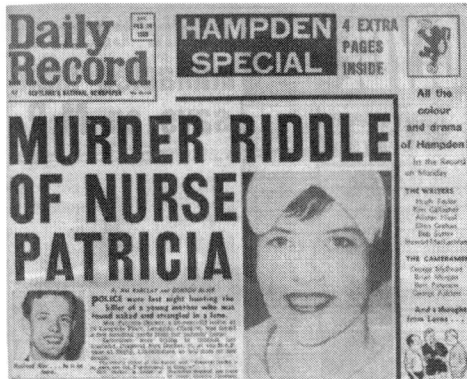

Front page of the Daily Record on Saturday 24th February.

John Wilson told police that Patricia had been planning to go dancing at the Majestic Ballroom on the evening she died and that was there they initially focused their enquiries. They found a witness who remembered dancing with Patricia at the Majestic, but several days later he told that he was mistaken and had got the night wrong. It wasn't until several days later that it was realized that Patricia had gone on to the Barrowland Ballroom and by the time that police began questioning potential witnesses there, people's memories had understandably faded. Recalling a stranger in a crowded dance hall wouldn't be easy in any circumstances, but several days after the event, it was virtually impossible. Some people remembered seeing an attractive, petite woman in a yellow dress dancing, but no-one could remember seeing her leave.

The distance from the Barrowland Ballroom to the lane

where Patricia's body was found is around three miles by the most direct route – about an hour at a brisk walk. No witness could be found who recalled seeing the young woman walking on the most likely route, so it was thought possible that she had taken a taxi or had been given a lift by someone. Extensive police enquiries failed to identify any taxi driver who had taken a fare in the right area at the right time and the working assumption was that Patricia had either accepted a lift from someone she had met at the ballroom who had driven her from the Barrowlands towards Langside Place or that she had walked home, either on her own or accompanied by her killer but that she had not been seen (it was a bitterly cold night and there were few people on the streets in the early hours, so this was thought to be possible).

A search by police divers of White Cart Water, a small river around one hundred meters from where Patricia's body was found, located her brown handbag and her bracelet but her yellow dress, grey duffel coat and underclothes were never found. Her watch casing was found in a puddle close to her body. An autopsy was performed by Dr. Gilbert Forbes of the University of Glasgow Medical School. This concluded that Patricia had been severely beaten about the head, probably by being punched and kicked and that her death had been caused by ligature strangulation. The ligature was not found and it was surmised that this might have been a belt or strap. The autopsy did not find any conclusive evidence of sexual assault.

The autopsy set the time of death at shortly after midnight, soon after she was believed to have left the Barrowland Ballroom. Patricia had been menstruating at the time of her death and a sanitary pad had been found close to her body. Police assumed that Patricia had met someone at the Barrowland Ballroom and had left with him, possibly accepting a lift in his vehicle or walking with him. He then took her back towards her parents' house at Langside Place, but had instead taken her into the lane off Carmichael Place where he had beaten her, removed her clothing and then strangled her.

Posters were placed across Glasgow following the murder of Patricia Docker including this one sponsored by the Daily Record newspaper.

It was assumed that the killer then went south, towards White Cart Water where he dumped her handbag and bracelet. This is a small river which can't be heard from the murder scene, which made detectives wonder whether the killer was familiar with this area? Police also wondered why the killer had dumped the handbag in the river. Was this because he knew that a leather bag was a potential source of fingerprints? After its immersion in the river, the handbag yielded no fingerprints and no prints were recovered from the crime scene. Likewise Patricia's missing clothing – did these have potentially incriminating blood stains on them and did the killer remove them to protect himself or were they taken as macabre souvenirs?

Inevitably, police initially considered Patricia's husband Alex as a potential suspect, but he was quickly ruled out when it was discovered that he had been at RAF Digby in Lincolnshire, more than two hundred and fifty miles away, at the time of the murder. With almost no other clues with which to work and no viable suspects, the police enquiry scaled down within weeks. Interviews with witnesses at the Barrowland Ballroom had failed to produce a good description of any of the men she had been seen with. The murder enquiry was never formally closed, but without any clues as to the identity of Patricia's murderer, there was very little that could be done. Then as now, police time and resources are limited and these were generally switched to cases which had a higher probability of being solved.

Chapter 2: Jemima McDonald

Eighteen months after the murder of Patricia Docker, another young mother set out for a night of fun and dancing at the Barrowland Ballroom. Jemima McDonald was thirty-two years old, slim, attractive and, just like Patricia, she loved to dance. Jemima (who friends called 'Mima') had three children – a twelve year old daughter and sons of nine and seven. Mima lived in a tenement building at 15 MacKeith Street in Bridgeton, to the east of the city centre ad not far from the Barrowland Ballroom. On the same landing lived her sister Margaret, and on Saturday August 16th 1969, Margaret had agreed to look after Mima's children while she went dancing. This was the third night in a row that Mima had gone out dancing – Margaret had also looked after the children on the previous Thursday and Friday nights.

Mima gave her children their tea and then dropped them off with Margaret and chatted with her sister briefly before leaving for the city centre. She was wearing a black pinafore dress, white blouse, off-white sling-back shoes and a warm brown coat. Mima had recently had her hair dyed and styled and it was still in curlers when she dropped off her children. She covered the curlers with a headscarf and told her sister that she didn't plan to take them out until she arrived at the ballroom so that her hair would look as good as possible.

Mima went to the ballroom alone. The problem, she told Margaret, was that many of her friends were married, and no longer wanted to out for a night of dancing, so she often went out by herself. She was looking forward very much to attending the popular over-25s night at the Barrowland. Before going to the ballroom, Mima stopped in at Betty's Bar on the Gallowgate, just one hundred meters from the ballroom. At that time, the Barrowland Ballroom didn't serve alcohol, and many patrons of the ballroom would call into local bars first. Some patrons in Betty's Bar remembered her talking with a tall, slim, red-haired young man in a suit.

When she arrived at the ballroom, it was thronged with dancers – Saturday night was the busiest night of the week and anything up to two thousand people were believed to have visited the Barrowland Ballroom that night. Despite the crowds, several people later remembered seeing Mima there and some remembered her being with one man in particular. He stood out, they said, because he didn't seem to belong. He had unfashionably short hair, for one thing, and he was wearing a good quality suit with a white shirt (one witness even recalled that the suit had *hand-stitched lapels*). These things contrasted with most young men at the ballroom that evening who sported longer hair and more casual dress. From the descriptions, this seemed likely to be the same man who Mima had been seen talking with earlier in Betty's Bar, but no-one recognized him or could remember seeing him at the ballroom before.

When the ballroom closed at midnight, Mima was seen leaving with the young man. It appeared that they planned to walk together back to Mima's home and several witnesses saw them as they walked together. They were seen to walk a short distance down Gallowgate before turning right on to Bain Street and then left on to the busy London Road which itself leads on to the A74, one of the main routes to the east of Glasgow. They were seen together on London Road at about 12:15am and again at around 12:30am as they walked together east along London Road before turning off on to a short-cut along Landressy Street. It was assumed that they then crossed James Street and entered MacKeith Street where Mima's flat was located. The distance from the Barrowland Ballroom to Mima's flat is less than one mile and the walk should have taken the couple around twenty minutes. But Mima never came home.

***

When Mima didn't come to collect her children on Sunday morning and no-one answered knocking on her flat door, Margaret became very worried. Later on the Sunday, she became even more concerned when she heard some local children talking about '*the body in the tenement.*' Less than thirty meters from the tenements in which Margaret and Mima lived was a dilapidated and abandoned tenement building at 23, MacKeith Street. The council had boarded up the ground floor windows and secured the door, but some of the boarding had been broken away and during the day, the empty building was used as an impromptu playground by local children. At night it provided shelter for vagrants and a place for prostitutes to take their customers. Most respectable local people avoided the sinister building.

By Monday, Margaret was very worried indeed about Mima, and she recalled what she had heard the children saying. She plucked up courage and went towards the dark and evil smelling empty tenement building at 23, MacKeith Street. She was surprised to find several local people inside and outside the empty building. It seemed that other people had also heard rumours that there was a body there. Margaret made her way inside. At first she couldn't see anything in the semi-darkness. Then someone pointed out what at first appeared to be a mannequin from a shop-window display lying in a bed-recess by one wall. Then Margaret noticed that the mannequin was wearing a torn black pinafore dress and a white blouse. And that its face was covered in blood. Mima MacDonald wasn't missing any more.

Detectives arrived quickly and it was ascertained that Mima

had been savagely beaten around the head and face before being raped and strangled with one of her own stockings. Her black patent leather handbag and her headscarf were missing though all her other clothes were found at the crime scene. A search by police of waste ground close to the derelict tenement failed to turn up the missing items. Local people had arrived at the empty tenement before the police and at least one had moved the body in an attempt to identify the dead woman, compromising the crime scene. An autopsy confirmed the cause of death and noted that Mima had died in the early hours of Sunday morning. It also added the fact that Mima had been menstruating at the time of her death and that a sanitary pad was found discarded close to her body.

Extensive door-to-door enquiries in the area produced little helpful new information. One woman who lived in MacKeith Street told police that she thought that she had heard a woman scream on the night that Mima was murdered, but she couldn't be sure of the time. One witness claimed to have seen a woman who resembled Mima talking to a man outside the abandoned tenement at around 12:40am on the night that Mima was murdered but it could not be definitely ascertained that this was Mima.

Because it was known from the outset that Mima had spent the evening at the Barrowland Ballroom, police immediately began questioning other people who had been there. Starting from Monday August 18th, the management of the ballroom began making announcements requesting anyone who had been there on Saturday night and might have seen Mima should contact the police. The following Saturday, August 23rd, police staged a re-enactment of Mima's walk towards her home from the ballroom using a policewoman dressed in similar clothes. This produced no new witnesses who had seen the couple as they walked from the ballroom towards MacKeith Street.

The similarities between the still unsolved murder of Patricia Docker and the murder of Mima MacDonald were obvious: both were murdered after spending the evening at the Barrowland Ballroom, both were beaten and strangled, both had been menstruating at the time of death and in both cases the dead women's handbags were removed from the scene. Newspapers picked up on this and on 21st August a senior detective from Glasgow City Police told a reporter that: *'There are one or two similarities between both murders...I cannot say more on that point at the moment.'*

Police enquiries had provided a good description of the man who Mima had spent the evening with from several witnesses. He was said to be between twenty-five and thirty five years of age with sandy or red hair (though some witnesses recalled his hair as being auburn or even dark), slim, pale-faced, smartly dressed and very tall – some witnesses remembered him as being over six feet tall. No-one recognized the man, though several said that they were confident that they could pick him out if they saw him again.

More than a week passed and the police still had no viable suspects for Mima's murder. The head of the City of Glasgow Police CID, Detective Chief Superintendent Tom Goodall, dubbed '*Glasgow's Maigret*', by the press, decided to try something different: he approached George Lennox Paterson, Deputy Director of the prestigious Glasgow School of Art. Lennox Paterson was mainly known as an illustrator, but he was also an accomplished portrait painter and Goodall asked him if he would be willing to create a painting of the man seen with Mima MacDonald at the Barrowland Ballroom? The portrait was to be based on a composite of witness descriptions of the man. This would be the first time in the history of Scottish criminal investigation that such a thing had been done and Goodall had to approach the Crown Office in Edinburgh for permission. When this was agreed, he contacted Lennox Paterson who rapidly produced a portrait. This was released to the press on Tuesday August 26th, ten days after Mima's murder.

The publication of what was said to be the face of Mima's

killer caused a sensation – the talent of Lennox Paterson produced not just a likeness, but a portrait of a man wearing an expression of cold, mocking hauteur. To most people it seemed that with such a clear image of the man's face in circulation, it was no more than a matter of time before the killer was apprehended.

George Lennox Patterson's portrait of the suspect in the murder of Mima McDonald.

Unfortunately the initial interest caused by publication of the portrait produced no new leads and no suspects. Police enquiries continued, but with little tangible evidence to go on, they made no progress. Mima MacDonald's three brothers and three sisters together raised one hundred pounds (a considerable sum in 1969) which they offered as a reward to anyone who could help to identify her killer. Even this failed to generate any new leads.

Then, just two months later, he struck again.

Chapter 3: Helen Puttock

Twenty-nine year old Helen Puttock also loved dancing, but just like Patricia Docker and Jemima MacDonald, the presence of two young children made it difficult for her to get out as often as she'd like. Helen had met her husband George while visiting her brother in Surrey and the couple had two sons, one of five and the other just one. George was a serviceman and Helen had initially followed him on his postings, including a long period in Germany. However, she hadn't enjoyed army life, finding herself lonely and isolated, and by 1969 she had returned to Glasgow to live with her mother and her two children at 129, Earl Street in the Scotstoun area of the city, to the west of the city centre.

George decided that he would apply for a posting closer to Glasgow but, in the meantime, Helen and George kept in touch by letter and George spent any leave he had in Glasgow with his wife and children. He was home on leave on Thursday October 30th, 1969 when Helen announced that she planned going dancing that evening with her older sister, Jeannie Langford. Initially, George wasn't too happy with this arrangement, telling Helen that he wasn't sure it was appropriate for a married woman to go out dancing without her husband but Helen reassured him that she simply wanted the chance to have a bit of a dance with her sister. He finally agreed and gave her ten shillings in order to take a taxi back home afterwards.

At around eight o'clock that evening, Helen and Jeannie left to catch a bus towards Glasgow Cross. Helen was wearing a black sleeveless dress, black shoes and a fake-fur ocelot coat and carrying her red handbag. She seemed very happy to be going out and assured George that she'd be back in reasonable time. When they arrived in the city centre, Helen and Jeannie visited a few pubs before meeting up with two friends, Marion Cadder and Jean O'Donnell, at the Trader's Tavern on Stevenson Street, just fifty meters from the Barrowland Ballroom. Then, the sisters joined the queue for the over-25 night in the ballroom – as usual for a Thursday night, the queue was long and none of the women there seemed unduly perturbed about the murder of Jemima MacDonald ten weeks earlier.

Once they had paid the four shilling admission fee and gone inside at around ten o'clock, it didn't take long for Jeannie to meet a man who seemed keen on being her dancing companion for what remained of the evening. He told her his name was John and that he lived in the Castlemilk area of the city, but she noticed that he didn't offer any other information about himself. She wondered if this was because he was married? She didn't really mind because all she wanted to do was dance and she had noticed that Helen also seemed to have found a companion, a tall, slim young man who seemed *'suave and a little sophisticated.'*

The two women happily danced with their partners, meeting for a chat now and again. Jeannie noted that Helen's partner wasn't much of a dancer, *'more of a shuffler,'* she said later. The two men they were dancing with also met, and the women laughed when it turned out that both were called John, though Jeannie later said that she didn't think that was either man's real name:

> *'I don't believe either of them were called John, in fact the man I was dancing with was first to introduce himself to the others. When it came to Helen's partner he seemed to pause for a second or two before giving his name as John, he seemed a bit apprehensive and it was the only time I saw him look less than confident because he seemed so certain of himself in every other way.'*

At around eleven-thirty the dancing finally ended and the two couples made their way towards the exit. Jeannie stopped to buy cigarettes at a machine in the upper foyer, but when she inserted her two shillings, nothing happened. Helen's partner became irritated by this and insisted on calling the manager and demanded that he give Jeannie her money back. Jeannie described *'John's'* attitude later:

'He wasn't outraged or shouting, he was collected and very calm but very assertive. It was like a schoolteacher speaking to a young child, he was giving the manager a real dressing down. I expected him to get a good hiding for the way he spoke to the manager, but to my surprise nothing happened and the manager seemed to back off.'

The manager agreed that the machine seemed to be faulty but explained that he couldn't give Jeannie a refund as all the tills had been cashed up for the night. However, he told her that if she returned the following day, he would see that she got her money back.

As the four made their way downstairs, Helen's John seemed to become angry and Jeannie heard him say *'My father says these places are dens of iniquity.'* Jeannie's John went to get his coat and, while they waited for him, Jeannie noted that Helen and her John were in conversation and she thought that John had said something to Helen which she didn't believe, because she was laughing and shaking her head. Then, the man produced something from a jacket pocket, perhaps a card or some form of identification, and showed it to Helen. Jeannie tried to see what it was, but then man put it quickly back in his pocket, saying *'You know what happens to nosy folk!'*

The four left the ballroom and began to walk together along

Gallowgate towards Glasgow Cross where taxis waited. When they arrived, Jeannie's John continued walking towards the city-centre, telling them that he intended to catch the late bus towards Castlemilk from George Square. Helen, Jeannie and John got into a taxi and began the twenty minute trip back to Scotstoun. Helen noted that John's attitude seemed to have changed – he was plainly irritated that Jeannie had accompanied him and Helen in the taxi and Jeannie assumed that he had hoped to be alone with her younger sister.

Jeannie tried to engage him in conversation by asking questions about him. He said little beyond noting that he liked golf and that his family owned a caravan in Irvine, southwest of Glasgow on the Firth of Clyde coast. He also mentioned that he had been fostered as a young child. When Jeannie asked if he liked dancing, his answers became rather odd. He told her that he didn't like the idea of married women going ballrooms and he seemed to become angry as he spoke of his dislike of 'adulterous women.' When Jeannie asked him what he had planned for the New Year, he answered that he didn't drink but preferred to spend his time in payer instead.

When the taxi arrived at Earl Street, Jeannie expected John and Helen to get out before it took her on to her home on Kelso Street, around one and a half miles further on.

Instead, John insisted that the taxi went first to Kelso Street where Jeannie got out, telling Helen that she would see her the following week but John slammed the taxi door closed while she was speaking and told the driver to take them to on to Earl Street. The driver later told police that he stopped outside 95, Earl Street (Helen's home was at 129, Earl Street) where Helen got out and walked in the direction of her home. She seemed, the driver said, angry and walked away without looking back. The male passenger paid the fare, got out and followed Helen down the street. The time was around 12:30am – 12:45am.

At around 02:00am, a Number six night service bus was travelling towards the city centre on Dumbarton Road when it stopped between Gardner Street and Fortrose Street (around two and a half miles closer to the city centre than Earl Street) to pick up a single male passenger. The driver, conductor and another passenger noted that the man looked as if he had been in a fight – his jacket was muddy and he had a scratch below one eye. The man seemed embarrassed by his appearance and a short time later, at the junction of Dumbarton Road and Derby Street, he stopped the bus and got off.

**

At 07:30 the following morning, Archibald MacIntyre, who lived at 95, Earl Street, took his dog out into the enclosed

36

yard behind the tenement buildings. Immediately, the dog began sniffing at what MacIntyre initially thought was a bundle of rags laying on the ground. He went closer, and saw that it was the body of a woman, her face covered in blood. He raced to the nearest telephone box and called the police.

When they arrived, they found the body of a woman, her face so badly beaten as to be unrecognizable and with a pair of stockings tightly knotted round her neck. Her clothes were torn and a gold chain she had been wearing was lying next to her. It was clear that this was murder and a Glasgow City Police incident caravan was set up outside the door of 95, Earl Street.

During the morning, a man arrived at the incident caravan saying that he was worried about his wife Helen who had gone dancing the night before at the Barrowland Ballroom but hadn't returned. Detective Superintendent Joe Beattie, the man assigned to lead the murder enquiry, took him inside the caravan. The man explained that he was George Puttock and said that he was worried about Helen. Beattie asked George what his wife had been wearing when she had gone out? George described Helen's clothes to the detective. Beattie put his hand on George Puttock's shoulder and said: *'I'm sorry son, your wife's been murdered.'*

Chapter 4: The Dapper Dancer of Death

An autopsy confirmed that Helen Puttock had been beaten, raped and strangled. The autopsy also confirmed that she had been menstruating at the time of her death and that someone, presumably her killer, had placed her sanitary pad underneath her armpit. Bite marks were also found on her arm. A stain on her tights was found to be semen and the sample was kept for further analysis. A search of the enclosed yard where her body had been found turned up a cheap cuff-link lying in the mud. Police speculated that this might have been torn from the murderer's clothing. One thing that wasn't found was Helen's red handbag.

When Jeannie Langford heard about her sister's murder, she was distraught and it was some time before she could talk t police. When she did, it quickly became clear that she was a vital witness. She had spoken with the main suspect several times during the evening and had even shared a taxi with him and Helen. During questioning she gave a description of John and recalled additional details not mentioned by other witnesses. He had good teeth, she remembered, but two of his front teeth were crooked and overlapped and a tooth on the upper right side was missing. She also remembered that he was wearing some form of metal badge on the lapel of his jacket and that he often rubbed this, as if it was somehow important to him. She thought that he had said in the taxi that his surname was 'Templeton' or 'Sempleson.' Jeannie's evidence was widely publicised, but for some reason the police identified this vital witness as 'Jeannie Williams', possibly to protect her identity from reporters.

On November 4th 1969, the Glasgow Herald ran a front-page story with the headline 'Bible Quoting' Man Sought By Murder Hunt Police.' This included the following description of the man Jeannie Langford had described:

> 'A man aged between 25-30, 5ft10 to 6ft tall, of medium build, with light auburn reddish hair, styled short, and brushed to the right. He had blue grey eyes, nice straight teeth with one tooth on the upper right jaw overlapping the next tooth, fine features, and is generally of smart modern appearance. He is dressed in brownish, flecked single breasted suit, the jacket of which has three or four buttons and high lapels. He has a knee length brownish coat of tweed or gabardine, a light blue shirt and a dark tie with red diagonal stripes.'

However, it was John Quinn, at that time the crime reporter working for another Glasgow newspaper, the Evening

Times, who provided the name which has become indelibly associated with this killer. He rushed from a police press conference about the murder to his car, which was equipped with a radio-phone. He called his editor with the story and, almost as an afterthought, added: '*Let's call him Bible John.*' The name stuck and the legend of Bible John, the religion obsessed serial killer, became part of Glaswegian and Scottish folklore. Quinn was later asked what made him choose this name for the killer. He said: '*I did not do it – as was said later in some books on the subject- because of a flair for the dramatic. I did it merely as the seemingly perfect tag to jog the memory of those whose paths may have crossed with the dapper dancer of death who made criminal history by being the first man to have an identikit picture issued with the approval of the Scottish Office.*'

Initially, police were very confident about catching Bible John. When Jeannie Langford was shown the painting done after the murder of Mima MacDonald by George Lennox Paterson, she said: '*My whole inside just churned. To me the resemblance was there. When I looked at it, it's a funny feeling, it's like something just turns in your guts, you know, it's like a wee kind of shiver of something. When I saw that I thought, God, that's a terrific resemblance!*' This was extremely important because it seemed to confirm that the killer of Mima MacDonald and Helen Puttock were the same man. Jeannie spent time with Lennox Paterson who made small changes to the painting following her instructions. The revised and full colour version of the painting was sent to the press and appeared in a number of Scottish newspapers and television news shows.

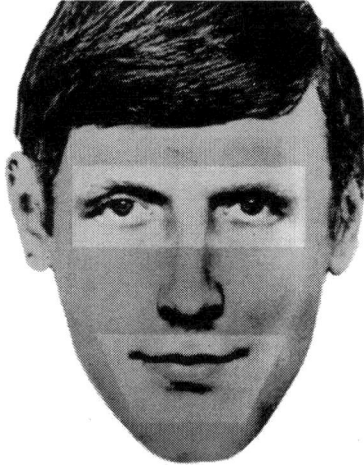

The Photofit image of Bible John produced with the help of Jeannie Langford.

Jeannie also worked with Glasgow City Police Photofit technicians to produce another version of the face of Bible John and the features on this composite image were very similar to those on the painting created by Lennox Paterson. With such striking and seemingly accurate pictures of the killer plus what the police knew about him through talking to witnesses, it seemed very unlikely that he could escape detection for long. Posters featuring the face of

Bible John appeared all over Glasgow and further afield – because of his short, neat hair and the fact that some witnesses had noticed that he wore a type of watch favoured by servicemen at the time, it was considered that Bible John might be in the armed forced. His picture and description were circulated to British Army bases and Royal Navy ships and bases around the world. Scottish newspapers ran the story of Bible John as front page news - *THE DANCE HALL DON JUAN WITH MURDER ON HIS MIND* was just one of the headlines relating to this killer and most newspapers adopted the name first suggested by John Quinn – Bible John.

Many, many people responded to the police appeals for information and identified a bewildering array of men as being Bible John, mainly on the basis of a resemblance to the painting and Photofit. Detectives investigating Helen Puttock's murder spent a great deal of time following up these leads, but none led to a viable suspect. Jeannie Langford attended many line-ups, but failed to identify Bible John. She also accompanied police to a number of locations to surreptitiously look at men who had been identified as resembling the portrait, but she failed to identify any of them as the man her sister had spent the evening with.

A team of fourteen police officers and two policewomen staked out the Barrowland and other dance halls across Glasgow. They focused on *'over-25 nights'* but their efforts failed to identify a single viable suspect, though many of them found that their dancing improved: one officer told a reporter that *'when this inquiry started, I could hardly dance a step. Now I get better every week.'*

Other detectives spent time analyzing British military and NATO records. The gap between the murder of Patricia Docker and Mima MacDonald was eighteen months – could this be because the killer had been posted abroad during this period? This line of enquiry failed to locate a single suspect. Detectives also spoke to more than fifty tailors in and around Glasgow in the hope that one might recall a customer who had a brown-flecked single-breasted suit made or altered, but this didn't produce anything useful. A survey of dentists in the area produced a list of over five thousand men with overlapping upper front teeth. All were located and excluded from the enquiry.

One continuing strand of the enquiry was the search for the other John who had been present at the ballroom with Helen, Jeannie and Bible John. This person hadn't come forward, despite extensive publicity, which made police believe that Jeannie's idea that he was a married man using a false name was correct. Police spent a great deal of time looking for this man, who became known as '*Castlemilk John*' because that was where he said that he was catching a bus to when he left the others. Detective Superintendent Joe Beattie, the man who led the Bible John enquiry, later told a reporter:

> '*One of my biggest regrets is that Castlemilk John never came forward. That was a bad break in the investigation. He would have been able to help. He was in Bible John's company that night. He may know something about the killer that would identify him. Bible John might have said he was a member of a golf club. Or where he lived or worked. Or what his hobbies were.*'

Despite an extensive investigation in the Castlemilk district in the south of Glasgow, this man was never found. Police also pursued other more tenuous lines of enquiry. Jeannie Langford had recalled that, in the taxi, Bible John had spoken about golf and he had mentioned being present when his cousin achieved a hole-in-one. Police visited over four hundred golf courses across Scotland in the hope that someone might remember a player scoring a hole-in-one while accompanied by a tall, red-haired man. None did. Dozens of churches were visited in the hopes that Bible

John might be a member of the congregation. He wasn't.

There was no shortage of leads – detectives took over fifty thousand witness statements and enquires extended as far as Hong Kong and America. None led to a viable suspect though over one thousand men were identified, interviewed and subsequently eliminated from the enquiry. The search for Bible John was the biggest manhunt ever undertaken by a Scottish Police force – at one point, over one hundred detectives and police officers were directly involved in the enquiry. All this effort led absolutely nowhere.

In early 1970, the Scottish Daily Record newspaper paid for Dutch psychic and parapsychologist Gerard Croiset to visit Glasgow to help in the search. Croiset had allegedly helped the Dutch police in murder and missing persons enquiries and he had gained considerable publicity in January 1970 when he had made predictions during the investigation of the kidnapping of Muriel McKay in England (despite Croiset's involvement, Mrs McKay's body was never found). Croiset told the Daily Record that Bible John lived in the Govan area of Glasgow and he provided a detailed description of the killer's house. Police did attempt to use this information, but it didn't produce a suspect and most felt that it was a waste of time.

Inevitably, when it didn't produce a result, the police

investigation into the Bible John murders began to wind down. No police service can afford to continue to employ the sort of resources used by Glasgow City Police during this investigation for an extended period of time. Despite all the leads, all the work and all the effort, police charged no-one with any of the murders and didn't even seem to have uncovered a single viable suspect.

In 1972, Detective Superintendent Joe Beattie spoke about the case:

> 'It is quite incredible that this man has eluded us. I am positive this man comes from Glasgow or nearby. He is between 25 and 30, between 5 ft 10 in and 6 ft tall, has light red hair, good features, blue-grey eyes and a smart modern appearance. ...there must be many people who know someone who looks like this artist's impression.'

Beattie also ruefully summed up his view the police failure to find Bible John in a later interview given after his retirement in 1976:

> 'Sometimes you get the ones you shouldn't get and you don't get the ones you should. This was one we should have got. We knew so much about him. There he was, with his short haircut, his meticulous dress

style, the patronising manner he had towards
women. I guess he lived west of a line from Stirling
to Lanark. He was either a serviceman or an ex-
serviceman.'

Glasgow City Police ceased to exist in 1975 when it was absorbed during the creation of the much larger Strathclyde Police. That force was itself subsumed into a single Scottish Police force, Police Scotland, in 2013. Despite that, the investigations into the murders of Patricia Docker, Mima MacDonald and Helen Puttock remain officially open. In 2018, a Police Scotland spokesperson said: *'The murders of Helen Puttock, Jemima MacDonald and Patricia Docker remain unresolved. However, as with all unresolved cases, they are subject to review and any new information about their deaths will be investigated.'*

The Police investigation into the murder of Helen Puttock noted a possible link with just two other murders: those of Patricia Docker and Mima McDonald. These are generally identified as the only three victims of Bible John. There have been suggestions that there may have been other victims of the same murderer, but I have not been able to find any other murders in the UK, solved or unsolved, which are so similar that they suggest that the same murderer may have been involved.

Part 2: Suspects

'It is quite incredible that this man has eluded us.'

Joe Beattie

Chapter 5: John White and John McInnes

Retired police detective Les Brown worked on the original Bible John investigation and in 2005 he published his autobiography, *Glasgow Crimefighter: The Les Brown Story*. In one chapter of this book, Brown discussed a man who gave his name as *'John White'* to the police during the Bible John investigation. Brown was present when the man was arrested in late 1969 outside the Barrowland Ballroom following an altercation with a woman. Brown and other officers noted the man's resemblance to the Bible John portrait and Photofit and took him to Marine police station. However, other police officers there said that it wasn't possible that he could be Bible John because he lacked the crooked teeth described by Jeannie Langford.

Brown's suspicions were further raised when it became known that the man had given a false name and address to the arresting officers – he was actually John Edgar from the Gorbals. In his book, Brown claimed that years later he spoke to another detective who had arrested a man at the Barrowland Ballroom in 1969 following a different fight there. The man had a head injury that required hospital treatment and he was taken there by police to whom he had given the name *'John White.'* However, when he was released from handcuffs, the man immediately ran away from the hospital and police. Brown claims that this man was also John Edgar and that, despite the lack of crooked teeth, he and other officers considered this man to be a viable suspect for the Bible John Murders.

John Edgar was twenty-seven in 1969, so his age is certainly within the age range described for Bible John. But, when Brown's book was published, the sixty-three year old Edgar contacted the press to make an irate rebuttal of these claims and to offer to provide DNA to allow him to be eliminated as a suspect. This was never done, but it doesn't seem likely that the real killer would make such an offer. Edgar was also interviewed by detectives following his arrest outside the Barrowland Ballroom and they were satisfied that he could not have been the killer. Overall, it seems unlikely that John White/Edgar is Bible John.

Another man interviewed by police during the initial Bible John investigation was John Irvine McInnes, a thirty-year old ex-soldier who had served as a Private in the Scots Guards and had then returned to Glasgow where he married and worked as a furniture salesman. He came from a family with a strong religious background, though he was also a gambler and a heavy drinker. McInnes was known to have been in the Barrowland Ballroom on 29th October 1969, the night before Helen Puttock met her killer, and he resembled the description of Bible John given by Jeannie Langford. The problem was, McInnes was put in more than one identity parade organized by the police, but Jeannie Langford and several other witnesses who had seen the man with Helen Puttock at the ballroom failed to pick him out. Some officers remained convinced that McInnes was a potential suspect, but even when pressed Jeannie was vehement that he wasn't the man – he didn't have crooked front teeth and his '*jug ears*' she said, were quite different to the man who had gone off in the taxi with Helen. Police also checked McInnes' clothes and found nothing similar to the suit that Bible John had been wearing on the evening Helen was killed. For these reasons, McInnes was eliminated as a suspect in 1969.

In 1980, John McInnes committed suicide by severing the brachial artery in his arm and bleeding to death. He was buried in Stonehouse cemetery in Lanarkshire alongside his father. In 1996, a cold case review of the Bible John case was carried out by Strathclyde Police. One of things being looked at was the possibility of using DNA to identify the killer of Helen Puttock. A small sample of semen and a hair, both presumably originating from her murderer, had been found on her clothing and these had been frozen and preserved during the initial enquiry. By 1996, new technology meant that it was possible to use DNA sampling to compare these samples with a sample taken from a suspect to definitively identify or rule them out. A bite mark had also been found on Helen Puttock's body and it was believed that casts and pictures of this could also be used to identify her killer. The cold case review looked again at John McInnes and his sister was persuaded to give a DNA sample to the police. The family hoped that this would finally exclude McInnes from the enquiry, but instead, it put him firmly in the frame. The sample from the sister was said to be an '*80% match*' with DNA extracted from the semen found on Helen Puttock's clothing, making it seem virtually certain that McInnes was the murderer.

Strathclyde Police passed this information to the Crown Office who approved an exhumation order on the body of John McInnes. On February 2nd 1996, in a welter of publicity, McInnes' body was removed from its grave in Stonehouse cemetery and taken to Glasgow University Medical Department. Detective Chief Inspector James McEwan of Strathclyde Police told reporters that he was '*very confident*' that the Bible John cases was finally about to be closed. Jeannie Langford disagreed – she was interviewed while the DNA testing was on-going and repeated her certainty that McInnes wasn't the man – she told a reporter: *'They think it's him, I don't. That's all there is to it.'*

Reporters waited for a follow-up announcement from Strathclyde Police. And waited. And waited. We now know that Jeannie Langford was right - DNA testing by police scientists failed to find a match between DNA recovered from McInnes' body and the sample taken from the Helen Puttock crime scene. The Procurator Fiscal then approved sending the samples to Department of Biological Anthropology of Cambridge University for further and more detailed testing. They in turn asked for assistance from the Institute of Medicine in Berlin. However many tests were done, it was apparent that there simply wasn't a DNA match. The scientists from Cambridge University finally noted that:

> 'The results of these DNA analyses provide no evidence to suggest that the semen stain or hair left near the body of Helen Puttock originated from John McInnes.'

The analysis of the bite mark also proved inconclusive. The body of John McInnes was found to have dentures. No dental records could be found, so nothing could be ascertained about when he received these or what his teeth looked like before he had dentures. In early July 1996, Strathclyde Police told the family of John McInnes that testing had definitively ruled him out as the killer of Helen Puttock.

This was an embarrassing admission for Strathclyde Police who had seemed very confident that McInnes was Bible John, especially when it was revealed that the exhumation and testing had cost the taxpayer almost one million pounds. The Shadow Home Affairs spokesman, Labour Member of Parliament for Dumbarton John McFall said: *'We know the police have a duty to investigate unsolved murders. This case seems to be a text-book example of how not to go about it.'*

The extensive and detailed DNA testing left no doubt: whoever Bible John was, he wasn't John Irvine McInnes. In 2005 Strathclyde Police conducted another review of the Bible John case and they asked up to ten men who had been interviewed at the time of the original enquiry to provide blood samples for DNA testing. This testing did not provide a match with the sample from Helen Puttock's clothing and scientists noted that the original samples had by that time deteriorated to the point where they were no longer useable for DNA comparison testing.

Chapter 6: Peter Tobin

In 2006, a man calling himself Patricia McLaughlin was working as a handyman at St Patrick's Roman Catholic Church in the Anderston area of Glasgow. Also working at the church as a cleaner was twenty-three year old Angelika Kluk, a student from Poland who was staying in the presbytery of the church. On 24th September, Kluk and McLaughlin were seen together at the church. Immediately after, both disappeared. On 29th September, police found Angelika Kluk's body hidden under floorboards under the church. She had been beaten, raped and stabbed.

At around the same time, police discovered that Patricia McLaughlin was really Peter Tobin, a man on the *Sex Offenders Register* after being convicted in 1994 of rape and assault and for whom an arrest warrant had been issued in November 2005 after he moved from Paisley without notifying police. Tobin was arrested in London soon after and in May 2007 he was sentenced to life imprisonment for the murder of Angelika Kluk after a trial at the High Court in Edinburgh.

Subsequently Tobin was also found guilty of the murders of fifteen year old Vicky Hamilton and eighteen year old Dinah McNicol after their bodies were found buried in the garden of a house at Irvine Drive in Margate in which Tobin had previously lived. Vicky Hamilton had last been seen in February 1991 and Dinah McNicol in August 1991. It was clear that Peter Tobin was a multiple murderer and there were suspicions that he might also be a prolific serial killer – he was said to have boasted of committing over fifty murders.

Tobin was originally from Glasgow and when it was discovered that he was a regular attendee at the Barrowland Ballroom in the late 1960s, people began to wonder whether he might also be Bible John? At first, the evidence looked compelling: His first wife, Margaret (who he met in the Barrowland Ballroom) described him as being a very smart dresser who was also capable of being charming. He was known to have used the alias *'John Semple'* on occasion, similar to the name *'John Sempleson'* which Jeannie Langford had heard Helen Puttock's killer using.

In 2010 a new book about Bible John was published, *The Lost British Serial Killer*, written by David Wilson and Paul Harrison. This claimed that Tobin was Bible John. David Wilson is a well known criminologist and a Professor of criminology at the Centre for Criminal Justice Policy and Research at Birmingham University. Wilson was certain that Peter Tobin was Bible John and he said in an interview: *'I am as convinced as it's able to be. As far as I am concerned the case is closed.'* Following publication of the book a woman named Julia Taylor came forward to say that she was certain that a smartly-dressed man who had behaved threateningly towards her at the Barrowland Ballroom in the late 1960s was Peter Tobin. Another woman came forward the same year to claim that Tobin had sexually assaulted her in the ballroom in 1968.

Photographs of Tobin as a young man at certainly seemed to have a resemblance to the portrait of Bible John and at around the time of the Bible John murders, Tobin had a tooth removed from his upper jaw, which detectives thought might account for Jeannie Langford's description of crooked teeth. Tobin had left Glasgow in late 1969, which might account for the sudden end to the killings by Bible John. Overall, Peter Tobin looked like a very good suspect and in 2006 Strathclyde Police started Operation Anagram, an attempt to connect Tobin with unsolved Scottish murders, including the Bible John killings.

Tobin, who is currently in prison with no prospect of ever being released, has steadfastly refused to co-operate with police. During one interview he was asked to provide information about other murders in order to put the minds of family members at rest. He replied: '*I don't give a fuck about them*' so the focus of the police team working on Operation Anagram was on collecting evidence from other witnesses. In terms of the Bible John killings, what they found didn't actually support the idea of Peter Tobin as Bible John.

First of all, one thing that all eyewitnesses seemed to agree on was that Bible John was noticeably tall. Most estimated his height at between 5' 10" – 6'. Some suggested that he was over six feet tall. Jeannie Langford was certain that he was tall because, she told police, she particularly noticed his teeth because her eyes were on a level with his mouth when she was talking to him. Peter Tobin is 5' 9". Most witnesses remembered Bible John as having red hair, but Tobin had fair hair.

In 1969, Peter Tobin was just twenty three. Most witnesses put the age of Bible John as twenty-five to thirty-five and the majority suggested that he was in his late twenties or early thirties. Perhaps most compellingly, when Jeannie Langford was shown a photograph of Peter Tobin taken in the 1960s by officers from Operation Anagram in 2006, she told them that she was certain that he was <u>not</u> the man that she and Helen had shared a taxi with.

Then there was the fact that Tobin was married to his first wife, Margaret MacKintosh at a Registry Office in Brighton on the 6th August 1969, ten days before the murder of Mima McDonald. His wife is certain that they remained together in Brighton until Tobin was arrested two weeks later by police officers from Glasgow who were looking for him in relation to a series of burglaries. He was driven back up to Glasgow in handcuffs on 20th August. This means that Tobin certainly can't be the killer of the second Bible John victim, Mima McDonald. Tobin also has a noticeable scar under his left eye, but no witness described Bible John as having such a scar and we know that Tobin had the scar when he met his first wife in 1969.

There are other factors which suggest that Tobin wasn't Bible John such as the fact that all Tobin's known victims were young women aged from fifteen to twenty-three (and the oldest, Angelika Kluk, looked much younger), while Bible John's victims were older with ages ranging from twenty-five to thirty two. All Bible John's victims were strangled while all the known victims of Peter Tobin were stabbed. The bodies of all Peter Tobin's victims were buried or hidden while there was no attempt to hide Bible John's victims. Of course, the methodology of a killer may change over time, but taking all these factors together, it seems very unlikely that Peter Tobin is Bible John.

Operation Anagram was wound down in 2011 without being able to find any information to conclusively link Peter Tobin with any murders other than those he had already been convicted for. The deterioration of the DNA extracted from Helen Puttock's murder scene meant that this couldn't be used to conclusively tie-in Tobin to this murder. However, in 2018 an amateur detective who identified himself only as '*Nate*' provided information to several Scottish newspapers as well as to Professor David Wilson and crime novelist Ian Rankin which he claims proves that Peter Tobin was Bible John. Nate claims that a man named Daniel Tobin was living in a flat on MacKeith Street, the street on which Mima MacDonald lived and on which the derelict house in which her body was found was located. Nate claims that Daniel Tobin was '*almost certainly*' Peter Tobin's cousin and that the murder of Mima MacDonald took place in that flat, though he has no evidence to support either claim and ignores the fact that Tobin's first wife has said that Tobin was with her in Brighton at the time of Mima McDonald's murder.

Nate also claims that Tobin murdered Helen Puttock in a flat at 107, Earl Street owned by an aunt of Helen Puttock. He notes that: '*Did Bible John fetch a mop and a pail after the deed? Of course he didn't. It must have been clear to everyone then, as it is now, that the locus of the crime was a private dwelling. She was murdered in a nearby house and her body dumped in the back courts of Earl Street. That's why there's no blood-strewn public crime scene.*' Nate seems to forget that Helen Puttock was strangled, something not likely to produce a '*blood-strewn*' crime scene in the yard behind 95, Earl Street where she was found and that an autopsy showed no evidence of her body being moved after death. Nate's claims attracted a surprising amount of attention when there seems little to commend them to anyone who has spent any length of time looking at these crimes.

As Tobin's first wife Margaret MacKintosh said in a newspaper interview of the idea that Peter Tobin was Bible John in 2011:

> 'In some ways, it would be convenient to learn he was Bible John as he is behind bars and it would give the families of the victims some closure. Tobin is a monster. I knew that then and tragically it's been proved to be true time and time again since. Bible John must also have been a monster — but I don't believe it is the same man.'

Perhaps it is comforting for us to believe that Peter Tobin must be Bible John? After all, no-one likes to believe that numbers of serial killers live among us. So, if a known killer was in Glasgow at the appropriate time, then surely he must be Bible John? Sadly, killers like Tobin are less rare than we might like to imagine and it is entirely possible that two multiple murderers were living in Glasgow at the same time in the late 1960s. There is certainly little evidence to support this idea and a number of things that suggest that it isn't true. There is no doubt that Peter Tobin is an evil man, but I don't think that he is Bible John.

Perhaps surprisingly, Peter Tobin is not the only Scottish multiple murderer who has been linked with the Bible John killings.

Chapter 7: Angus Sinclair

In October 2014 a man named Angus Robertson Sinclair was found guilty of the murders of two teenage girls, Christine Eadie and Helen Scott in Edinburgh in 1977. Sixty-nine year old Sinclair was sentenced to serve a minimum of thirty-seven years in prison, meaning that he will be one hundred and six years old before he will be eligible for parole. Initially, Sinclair's brother-in-law, Robert Hamilton, was also suspected of involvement in the murders, but he died in 1996 and so could not be tried.

However, this wasn't the first time that Sinclair had killed. When he was tried for the murders of Eadie and Scott (whose killing became known as the *'World's End Murders'* as the World's End, a pub in Edinburgh, was the last place they were seen alive) he was already serving a life sentence for the murder of seventeen year old Mary Gallacher in Glasgow in 1978.

His convictions for all three murders came about because of a cold-case review of unsolved Scottish murders but even when convicted of the murder of Mary Gallacher, he was already serving a life sentence for a string of rapes and sexual assaults on a number of children aged from six to fourteen.

Even Mary Gallacher wasn't Sinclair's first murder victim.

In 1961 Sinclair, aged just sixteen, was jailed for ten years after being found guilty of the culpable homicide and sexual assault of seven year old Catherine Greenhill. The judge at that trial described Sinclair as: *'obsessed with sex and, given the minimum opportunity, he will repeat these offences irrespective of what promises he may give to the contrary.'* The judge was right, but Sinclair was released on parole in 1967 after having served just six years. Many people believe that Sinclair was responsible for more murders than those he has been convicted of.

In a four month period in 1977, three women were murdered in or around Glasgow. Hilda McAuley, Agnes Cooney and Anna Kenny all disappeared after spending the evening in Glasgow. The bodies of all three were found bound, gagged, raped and strangled and dumped in remote areas.

Another woman, Frances Barker, was abducted in Glasgow in June 1977 and her body was found dumped in a remote lane in Glenboig in Lanarkshire. She too had been bound, gagged, strangled and raped. A lorry driver, Thomas Ross Young, was convicted of her murder and sentenced to life imprisonment. Young died in 2014, but he claimed that Angus Sinclair was the real murderer.

There are certainly links which strongly suggest that Sinclair may have been involved in these four murders. A

Scottish police review of unsolved murders in Glasgow in 1977 was carried out in 2004 and concluded that it was very likely that:

> *'Angus Sinclair and Gordon Hamilton are responsible for all the linked crimes. The circumstances of their deaths and the methods used to bind, restrain and kill them, have striking similarities, findings not matched in any other group, or indeed in any other individual.'*

However, the Crown Prosecution Service decided that there was insufficient evidence to bring charges against Sinclair for these other murders.

It seems very unlikely that a man who might have killed six women in a period of little more than eighteen months did not also kill others – Sinclair's ex-wife Sarah certainly thought it likely that he had been killing in Glasgow for a period of ten years or more. Perhaps inevitably, it has been suggested that Angus Sinclair may also be Bible John.

Sinclair was certainly living in Glasgow at the time of the Bible John murders and in some ways the murders he is believed to have committed are superficially similar to the Bible John killings – for example, Sinclair's victims were raped and strangled and at least one was strangled with her own stockings, as were at least two of Bible John's victims.

One of the people to suggest Angus Sinclair as a fit for at least one of the Bible John killings is Nate, the same amateur investigator who presented theories about Peter Tobin in 2018. Nate claimed to have discovered that Robert Hamilton, Angus Sinclair's future brother-in-law, was living in a house on Langside Place, the same street where Patricia Docker was living with her parents when she was murdered. Nate has used this to suggest that Sinclair, recently released from prison in 1968, might have killed Patricia. However, he hasn't produced any evidence to support this theory.

There are a couple of good reasons not to believe that Angus Sinclair had anything to do with the Bible John killings. Most notably, his appearance. Sinclair was very short at around 5' 6". There is simply no way that he could be described as tall, which is how most witnesses described Bible John. He also had a distinctive mop of dark, curly hair – very different to the neatly cut red hair of Bible John. The bodies of Sinclair's known and suspected victims were hidden, usually by being taken to remote areas and dumped. This didn't happen with any of Bible John's victims. All Sinclair's victims were bound and gagged, something that didn't happen to any of Bible John's victims.

It's not possible to completely rule out Angus Sinclair as a suspect in the murder of Patricia Docker, but the descriptions given by witnesses who saw the presumed murderer of Helen Puttock and Mima McDonald do seem to rule him out in those cases.

Overall, I don't think there is good evidence to suggest that Angus Sinclair is responsible for any of the Bible John murders.

Chapter 8: Bible John the Police Officer?

Almost from the beginning, there has been speculation that Bible John might have been a police officer. Partly this was because of his neat appearance and short hair at a time when many young men were going for a more casual look. It was also suggested that his ability to avoid detection was because, as a police officer, he knew precisely how the police investigation was being conducted and could more easily avoid being caught.

Then, in 2013, a book was written by an ex-police officer which claimed to have found new evidence proving that Bible John was indeed a police officer. *Dancing with the Devil* is written by Paul Harrison, a retired UK police officer who was one of the first British officers to cross-train with the FBI Behavioural Analysis Unit based in Quantico, Virginia. Harrison spent thirty years working as a police officer and most of that time as a detective in Northamptonshire. Since retiring in 1998 he has written more than thirty non-fiction books, mainly on the topic of crime and detection. He also gives talks on various aspects of crime writing as well as police methods and psychological offender profiling.

Harrison claims that he got the idea that Bible John was a

police officer from Joe Beattie – Beattie was the detective in charge of the Bible John investigation and he continued to work on this case until his retirement in 1976. Harrison claims that Beattie told him that he had come to believe that Bible John was a police officer early in the investigation, but that he was not allowed to pursue this line of enquiry. Harrison has told a Scottish newspaper that:

> 'When the most senior ranking officers in the force found out Beattie was beginning to investigate his own officers, he was ordered to shut his operation down. Beattie was a man of huge integrity, it shattered him to believe the killer was one of his own.'

Harrison went on to add more evidence to support the notion that Bible John was a police officer. For example, he claimed that Jeannie Langford saw the man her sister was with produce a police warrant card and that the manager at the Barrowland Ballroom also recognised the man who argued with him about the cigarette machine as an undercover police officer. Harrison further claims that, on more than one occasion, Jeannie Langford pointed out a man in Marine police station as being the person with who she and Helen had shared a taxi but Joe Beattie told her that she must be mistaken because the man was a police officer.

According to Harrison, Castlemilk John, the man with whom Jeannie Langford spent the evening dancing on Halloween 1969 was also an undercover police officer, though he does not produce convincing evidence to support this contention. Harrison claims that the police officer who was known to be Bible John by senior members of Glasgow City Police was persuaded to take early retirement and moved to the Highlands. Harrison further claims that he was able to find records of all police officers who retired soon after the Bible John killings and that he was able to identify the retired officer who was Bible John. Harrison also suggests that the man may have continued to kill and that unsolved murders in the Highlands should be investigated. For legal reasons, the ex-officer who Harrison claims was Bible John is not named in the book, but Harrison states that he passed all the relevant information to Strathclyde Police.

This all sounds interesting, but there are reasons to doubt that the case is quite as watertight as Harrison claims. First of all, Jeannie Langford's account of events in the ballroom on the night that Helen was murdered do mention the man with her sister producing something and showing it to Helen. However, Jeannie was sure that she didn't see what it was and when she tried to look, the man quickly put it back in his pocket. She certainly never seems to have told anyone at the time or subsequently that what he produced was a police warrant card. Likewise the claim that Jeannie identified Helen's killer as a police officer in the Marine police station – Jeannie was interviewed many times up to her death in 2010, and she never mentioned this to anyone else.

For example, Jeannie gave a detailed interview to Magnus Linklater of the Scottish Review about the Bible John case at the time of the exhumation of John McInnes in 1996. In this interview Jeannie specifically mentioned the card she had seen Bible John show to Helen and noted that it was pink in colour and perhaps some sort of military pass? She didn't mention in this interview (or in any other interview she gave) that this might have been a police warrant card or that she thought Bible John was a police officer or that she had ever seen him in the Marine police station. It seems more than odd that she would have told the author of *Dancing with the Devil* these things, but no-one else.

Joe Beattie was also interviewed many times on the subject of Bible John after his retirement in 1976. He discussed many theories (including the idea that John McInnes was Bible John) but at no time did he mention to any interviewer that he thought that Bible John was a police officer – the only thing he did say about Bible John to interviewers was that he thought he might be a serviceman or an ex-serviceman. Beattie was generally regarded as a man who was both entirely straight and very willing to state his beliefs and it does seem unlikely that if he really had been ordered to abandon the search for Bible John because the killer was known to be a police officer that he would not have told someone else about this. The Bible John murder enquiry was one of the largest, most expensive and longest running in Scottish Police history, but Paul Harrison would have us believe that this enquiry was undertaken while senior officers knew precisely who Bible John was. I find this difficult to believe.

Finally there was the expensive and embarrassing exhumation of John McInnes in 1996. Glasgow City Police was subsumed into Strathclyde Police in 1975 and members of Glasgow City Police transferred to the new force. It seems very hard to believe that, if senior officers of Glasgow City Police knew Bible John's real identity in 1970 that this would not also have been known within Strathclyde Police in 1996. Yet the actions of Strathclyde Police in 1996 strongly suggest that they truly believed that John McInnes was Bible John.

Overall, it's not possible to say with certainty that Bible John was not a police officer, but I don't find the evidence in *Dancing with the Devil* persuasive and I haven't seen any other convincing evidence that Joe Beattie or Jeannie

Langford believed this to be so.

Chapter 9: Other Suspects

Peter Sutcliffe

George Puttock, the husband of Helen Puttock, has said on more than one occasion that he believes that serial killer Peter Sutcliffe should be questioned about Helen's murder.

Peter William Sutcliffe was convicted in 1981 for the murder of thirteen women and the attempted murder of seven others. Sutcliffe, who had become known as the Yorkshire Ripper during the police hunt for him, had committed the killings in the Leeds and Bradford areas of England between 1975 and 1980. However Sutcliffe first came to the attention of West Yorkshire Police in September 1969 when he attacked a woman in Bradford by smashing her over the head with a stone in a sock. Sutcliffe was told by police that he was '*very lucky*' not be charged with assault over this attack.

Police suspect that Sutcliffe was involved in many more attacks than those he was convicted of, and perhaps more murders. As recently as 2017, police were looking at fifteen murders that Sutcliffe might have been involved in. One of these was the unsolved 1977 murder of Anna Kenny in Glasgow. At this time Sutcliffe was working as a long-distance lorry driver and he is known to have made regular trips from the Midlands to the General Motors plant at

Newhouse, around fifteen miles west of Glasgow. Overall the evidence suggests much more strongly that Anna Kenny was killed by Angus Sinclair, but is it possible that Peter Sutcliffe was Bible John?

Sutcliffe was twenty-three at the time of the murders in 1969, which puts him just outside the age range estimated by witnesses who described Bible John. He is known to have bludgeoned his victims and at least one was also strangled, which is at least similar to the killing of Bible John's victims.

However, Sutcliffe's job as a lorry driver didn't begin until 1975 and before that there is no record of his spending time in or around Glasgow before that date. Sutcliffe wasn't tall and he had dark, curly hair, not the red hair associated with Bible John. He had a distinctive Midlands accent and he generally wore a dark, neatly trimmed beard and photographs from late 1969 show that he had this beard at that time. It is very difficult indeed to see how the descriptions given by witnesses of Bible John could be of Peter Sutcliffe.

Given these things, it seems very unlikely indeed that Peter Sutcliffe could be Bible John, despite George Puttock's assertions.

'*Cracker*' finds a new Bible John suspect

Professor Ian Stephen is a consultant forensic psychologist who has been involved in criminal profiling for many years. He is also said to be the inspiration behind the character of Dr. Eddie '*Fitz*' Fitzgerald, a criminal psychologist played by actor Robbie Coltraine in the popular ITV television series '*Cracker*' from 1993 – 1996 (Professor Stephen was also an advisor for the show and '*cracker*' is a colloquial term for a criminal psychologist).

Professor Stephen provided advice to the team investigating the Bible John murders before his retirement. Then, in 2000, he was contacted by a Scot living in the US who had read about Stephen's work as a profiler on the Internet. The man said that he believed that one of his cousins might be Bible John. This man, who was still alive at that time and living in the south of England, was described as the son of a police officer who was raised by a very religious aunt. At the time of the murders he was married with two children and living just outside Glasgow.

Professor Stephen's contact said that the man resembled the Bible John portrait and loved dancing, often spending evenings at ballrooms in Glasgow. However, in the late 1960s his behaviour seemed to change and he began to spend more time away from his family, sometimes going out for the evening and not returning until the following day.

In early 1970, soon after the murder of Helen Puttock, this man sold his house in Glasgow and moved to England with his family. He was never questioned by police in relation to the Bible John murders. Professor Stephen admitted that the evidence was circumstantial, but said that: *'The profile appears to fit that of Bible John. I think the police have got to have a serious look at it.'* He told several newspapers that he had passed on what he knew to Lothian and Borders Police as soon as he received the information from the contact in America, though he didn't name the suspect in his newspaper interviews.

There was a brief flurry of interest in the press when Professor Stephen announced this apparent new suspect in the Bible John case, but nothing more emerged subsequently. The only comment from Strathclyde Police was: *'We will examine the correspondence delivered to Lothian and Borders police officers to establish if it represents additional information.'*

The lack of hard information makes it very difficult to say a great deal about this suspect but the circumstantial nature of the evidence doesn't make it seem very likely that Bible John has finally been identified. The lack of any further announcement from Strathclyde Police suggests that they did not find this new information compelling.

In the fifty years since the Bible John murders, many potential suspects have been identified, but for the reasons noted here, none of them seem to me to entirely fit the profile of Bible John. When a violent murderer such as Peter Tobin or Angus Sinclair is apprehended, it's tempting to try to ascribe other murders to them. However, I don't believe that the evidence supports the notion that any of the suspects detailed here are Bible John.

Part 3: Bible John

'Sometimes you get the ones you shouldn't get and you don't get the ones you should. This was one we should have got.'

Joe Beattie

Chapter 10: Building a Profile of Bible John

One technique used to learn more about a serial killer is to create a profile of the person. This is often done by investigators searching for an unknown offender and it is a technique first developed by the Behavioral Science Unit of the FBI in the US when investigating serial killers in the 1960s. Pete Klismet, a retired FBI Agent and criminal profiler has described the process in this way:

> *'Criminal profiling is the art of developing a behavioural profile of an offender based on evidence from a crime scene and many other factors involved in an investigation of a violent crime.'*

We have some information on the crime scenes associated with Bible John, so it may be possible to build a *deductive profile* of the killer - this is a profile based on the evidence associated with specific crimes. However, this can be combined with an *inductive profile* which uses statistical analysis of similar crimes and criminals. This process won't tell us who the killer is, but it may tell us more about him.

Profiles are often used when seeking serial killers, and Bible John is a serial killer. The definition of such a murderer is a person who kills three or more people over a period of more than one month with significant periods between each killing. Profiles of serial killer use psychology, but they also use common sense to establish facts about the killer by analyzing the evidence. Let's see if we can establish a basic profile of Bible John by looking at the things that are generally considered to be known about him.

He was from the Glasgow area. Some of the witnesses who had contact with Bible John commented that he appeared to have a Glasgow accent, though he spoke in a *'cultured'* or *'mannered'* way. None said that he had an accent from anywhere else. Where someone shares the same accent as a witness, this often won't be noticeable to that witness. Where a person has a different regional accent, that will generally be immediately apparent, even if many people find it very difficult to accurately identify particular British regional accents. No witness who heard him speak suggested that Bible John had an unfamiliar accent. The Glaswegian accent is very distinctive and this leads me to believe that, as the police suspected, Bible John originated in the Glasgow area.

He worked in a white-collar job. The vocabulary, manner of speech and manners of Bible John were commented on by several witnesses who noted that he seemed *'refined'* and *'a cut above the ordinary'* which made him seem as if he stood out from the majority of men at the

Barrowland Ballroom. Jeannie Langford noticed that he had neatly trimmed fingernails and smooth hands – not the hands of a manual worker. He wore good quality clothes and had short and neatly-trimmed hair. All these things suggest that he worked in a job where a professional, neat appearance was important.

He was used to people doing what he asked. The manager of the Barrowland Ballroom in 1969 was not a person with who many people argued. Scar-faced, tough and very willing to personally eject those he didn't like the look of, he was a slightly menacing presence. Yet, when Bible John remonstrated with him about the faulty cigarette machine, he meekly agreed to refund the cash the following day. Jeannie Langford described Bible John talking to him *'like a schoolteacher speaking to a young child.'* Bible John was, she surmised, a man who was used to people doing what he asked. This could suggest that he was a police officer, someone with a military background or even, as she suggested, a teacher. It could also mean that he was someone from a religious group or assembly where he had some leadership role or even someone from senior management in a commercial company where he was used to subordinates accepting his instructions.

He used the Barrowland Ballroom to find victims. It appears that Bible John met all his victims at the

Barrowland Ballroom. In the case of Mima McDonald, it is possible that he met her in a bar beforehand, and this may have been arranged in advance. In the case of Helen Puttock, he met her fortuitously at the ballroom. It's tempting to deduce from this that he regularly trawled the ballroom in search of victims, but this does not seem to have been the case. The witnesses who saw Bible John with Helen Puttock (which included the manager and other staff) all said that they didn't recognize him, which suggests that he wasn't a regular there. It does not seem likely that he was a habitual attendee at the Barrowland and, given the publicity following the murder of Helen Puttock, it does not seem likely that he returned there after the end of October 1969.

He had a detailed knowledge of several areas of Glasgow. I'm not so convinced by the evidence for this. It's certainly true that both Patricia Docker and Mima McDonald were murdered close to their homes and in areas that would not have been known to someone unfamiliar with the area – Patricia Docker's body was found in a secluded and inaccessible lane and Mima McDonald in a derelict house. These were ideal locations for murder, but it is possible that these locations weren't chosen by the killer. In these two cases, it seems at least possible to me that the two women took their new beau to these places for a quick kiss and a cuddle away from prying eyes. In the case of the murder of Helen Puttock, anyone who was familiar with tenement housing would have realized that there were enclosed yards behind and the murderer would not have needed advance knowledge of the area to realize this. The only evidence which seems to support the idea that Bible John had detailed local knowledge was his ability to find White Cut Water, the small river close to the scene of Patricia Docker's murder where he dumped some of her possessions. However, he may simply have taken these things from the crime scene with the intention of getting rid of them as soon as possible and ha may have then come across the river fortuitously. For these reasons, I don't think we can assume that Bible John must have had a detailed knowledge of the areas where he committed his murders.

He had a detailed knowledge of the Bible. This is part of what gave this killer his name - and alleged fascination with the Bible. However, it's worth bearing in mind that what we know of this aspect of his personality comes from one witness only and during a relatively short period of time. Jeannie Langford noted that the man that Helen had spent the evening with seemed to change after the confrontation over the faulty cigarette machine. As she, Helen, Castlemilk John and Bible John made their way towards the exit of the ballroom, she heard him say angrily

'*My father says that these places are dens of iniquity.*' This was the first time that she had heard him use any phrase that had a religious connotation.

Afterwards, in the taxi, Jeannie asked him whether he supported Celtic of Rangers, to which he made the odd reply '*I'm agnostic.*' When she asked him what he meant, he launched into a long quotation which she thought probably came from the Bible, possibly something about Moses and bulrushes though she couldn't be certain. This was the only time he quoted from the Bible. Jeannie said in a later interview: '*He came away with something, a reference to the Bible. I canna remember the exact words but it was something from the Bible. That was the only time – it was the papers that gave him that name.*'

From Jeannie's account of these conversations, Bible John received his soubriquet. But it seems that he only once quoted from the Bible, and even then, Jeannie wasn't certain about this. Many accounts of this killer suggest that he quoted extensively and often from the Bible, but a detailed reading of testimony indicates that this isn't true. Can we assume from this one quote that he was interested in or perhaps even obsessed by religion and the Bible? That's a long stretch, and even Joe Beattie, the detective in charge of the case, wondered just how great was this man's knowledge of the Bible? In an interview after his retirement he said: *'I do not think he is a very religious man, but just has a normal intelligent working knowledge of the Bible which he likes to air.'* I agree and I'm cautions about including knowledge of religion and/or the Bible as a factor in the profile of this killer. It's a possibility, but without more corroborating information I'm reluctant to take this as proved.

In addition to these points there also certain other things we can deduce about the killer from the crime scenes and the injuries to the victims. For example, there was no attempt to hide or cover any of the bodies, which generally implies that the killer did not feel ashamed of his actions, which may mean that he felt that the women he killed deserved what happened to them.

All three women were strangled with ligatures. Strangulation is often used in sexual murders where the killer can prolong the suffering of the victim in order to achieve sexual satisfaction. The ligature used in the case of Patricia Docker was not found, but was described as being *'a belt'* or something similar. Patricia was not wearing a belt when she left home, and I would suggest that what was used was more likely the strap of her handbag. The handbag was then taken from the scene and dumped in a nearby river, removing any possible fingerprint evidence. All Patricia's clothing was also removed from the scene, either because the killer wanted to ensure that there was no possibility of police acquiring fibre, hair or bloodstain evidence or because he wanted to keep them as souvenirs. This is known as 'controlling the crime scene' and it suggests that the killer had knowledge of police procedure. This could imply that he was himself a police officer, or it may indicate that he had offended before.

All three murdered women were menstruating at the time they were killed. In the murders of Patricia Docker and Mima McDonald, the women's sanitary pads were placed close to their bodies. In the case of the murder of Helen Puttock, her sanitary pad was placed under her arm. This placement of sanitary pads does not appear to be accidental and suggests that the fact that the women were menstruating was significant to the killer. Perhaps he had expected to have sex with the three women after spending the evening with them at the ballroom and when they tried to refuse because they were menstruating, he was overcome with murderous rage? This isn't completely unknown; one forensic psychologist has noted: 'In some men who are sexually immature, or have been rejected by women in the past, the menstrual period can trigger deep-seated feelings of disgust.'

All three women were badly beaten about the face and head. In the case of Mima McDonald and Helen Puttock, these injuries were so severe that both women were left unrecognizable. According to documentation from the FBI, these type of injuries are: *'not only a manifestation of deep-seated and often long-standing anger by the offender against the victim, but also an attempt to depersonalize him or her . . . the facial battery indicates an attempt to strip the victim of actual identity.'* It is possible that Bible John's anger and disgust were triggered when he realised that the women he had accompanied home were menstruating and they refused to have sex with him. It is also possible that anger felt by the killer may also have been because he believed that his victims were adulterous women who deserved to die – both Patricia Docker and Helen Puttock were married and Mima McDonald had three children, though she wasn't married at the time of her death.

All these things tell us that Bible John was a sexual sadist who vented a great deal of anger towards his victims and did not feel ashamed of his actions and who appears to have had some knowledge of police procedure. From this we can deduce that this killer was *'organized'*, as defined by the FBI system classification. The definition of an organized serial killer includes:

> *'Organized criminals are antisocial (often psychopathic) but know right from wrong, are not*

insane and show no remorse. They have some degree of social grace, may even be charming, and often talk and seduce their victims into being captured. Organized killers are very difficult to apprehend because they go to inordinate lengths to cover their tracks and often are forensically savvy, meaning they are familiar with police investigation methods.'

Statistically, organized serial killers are most likely to be of above-average intelligence, physically attractive, married or living with a domestic partner, educated and employed. They are also emotionally cold and manipulative and often arrogant, being convinced that they are more intelligent and capable than anyone else.

There are two further things that we need to consider in building this profile of Bible John as an organized serial killer. These are Modus Operandi (MO) and signature. The MO consists of the things the killer must do to commit their crimes – things like how they find victims, where they commit the murders and how they kill. The signature consists of actions that are not intrinsic to the commission of the crime but which serve the emotional or psychological needs of the killer.

In the case of Bible John, the MO is entirely consistent. Victims were located and identified at the Barrowland

Ballroom on an over-25 night (a location where, by repute, married women willing to have an affair were likely to be found). The killer spent time talking to his victims and gaining their trust to the point that they agreed to allow him to accompany them on the trip back to their homes. The killer then went with the selected victim to an isolated/inaccessible location close to their homes. When they had been brought to this location, or persuaded to go there, the killer would attack, most likely by punching and kicking the victims in the head.

When incapacitated and subdued by this initial attack, two of the victims were then raped, though there was no evidence of sexual assault in the case of Patricia Docker. They were then strangled to death with a ligature. In the latter two cases, the ligature was the women's own stockings. In the first murder we do not know what the ligature was, though as noted, it seems possible that this was the strap of Patricia Docker's handbag. When the women were dead, there was no attempt to conceal their bodies – they were simply abandoned in the place in which they were killed, though in the case of Patricia Docker, her clothes were removed and taken from the scene.

There are two main elements which make up the signature in this case. In each murder, a sanitary pad was taken from the victim and placed on or close to the body. This occurred in all three murders which means it is unlikely to be accidental and suggests that the sanitary pad itself or the fact that the murdered woman was menstruating was significant to the killer. In each murder, the victim's handbag was removed from the crime scene. In the case of the murder of Patricia Docker, this was recovered in a nearby river. In the other two cases, the victim's bags were never found. This <u>could</u> mean that these items were somehow significant to the killer and that perhaps the latter two were kept as souvenirs, though it could also be that the killer recognised handbags as a possible source of fingerprint evidence and simply wanted to remove these potential pieces of evidence.

Finally, we need to think about the circumstances of each murder. Although I have explained why I think this murderer belongs to the *'organized'* category of serial killers, I am not at all certain that he set out intending to murder his victims. The control of crime scenes suggests strongly someone who was familiar with police procedure, yet he had been seen by a number of witnesses with his victims. In the case of Helen Puttock in particular, he had been seen for an extended period by Jeannie Langford and Castlemilk John and had even drawn attention to himself in the incident involving the cigarette machine. These things make no sense at all if he was familiar with police investigative procedure and he had intended to kill Helen that night. He must have known that he had been seen with her and that it was very likely that he would be recognized and found. Most organized killers are very careful not to be seen with their victims if possible. It seems far more likely that something happened after he was alone with Helen to provoke his anger and caused him to explode in murderous rage.

This profile is helpful in understanding more about the personality and psychology of this murderer, but it is only truly useful if we have a suspect with which to compare the profile. However, in the search for this killer surely the most significant thing is that we know precisely what Bible John looked like.

Or do we?

Chapter 11: The Face of Bible John

'There must be many people who know someone who looks like this artist's impression.'

Joe Beattie

It's tempting to think of the human memory as a machine for recording and playing back experiences, a sort of super-video recorder, but that's not how it works. Instead, we unconsciously edit our memories, sometimes long after the event. For example, it's not uncommon for several people to have quite different memories of the same event. Each may be convinced that they are remembering what happened correctly and each would pass a lie-detector test without difficulty, but obviously the different versions cannot all be the objective truth. The unreliability of memory is a particular problem when investigating crime.

Eyewitness testimony is especially troublesome. A review of wrongful convictions in America in 1988 found that more than fifty percent were due to mistaken eyewitness identification, and those were just the cases which had been overturned in court – there is no way of assessing how often mistaken eyewitness identification is a factor in convictions which have not been overturned. Part of the problem is the way that our brains store information about faces. Research suggests that this done *'holistically'*, in other words, most people remember a general impression of a face rather than remembering the individual elements of that face.

In 2013, Graham Pike, Professor of Forensic Cognition at the Open University, wrote an essay called '*Photofit Psychology.*' In this essay he noted:

> '*Describing faces is difficult. Even describing the face of someone you know very well can be tricky. Try it if you don't believe me! I'm betting that you can describe their hair fairly well, but really struggle for most of their features. Describing the face of someone you are not familiar with, saw briefly and sometime ago is extremely difficult indeed.*
>
> *Try picturing a face in your mind and then try 'zooming' in on the nose; you will find it extremely hard, if not impossible, to do.*'

But, that's just what police technicians assembling a composite image must ask a witness to do. As would an artist like George Lennox Paterson who was trying to create a painting based on the descriptions of several witnesses. Identikit, the system in use by most British police forces in the late 1960s, was first introduced in America in the 1950s. The original Identikit system provided over five hundred drawings of different facial features on transparent acetate sheets. Witnesses were asked to look at each feature in isolation and from this the technician would assemble an image of a face. However, this relied on witnesses being able to recall individual facial features, something that we know people aren't generally particularly good at.

By the late 1960s, Identikit was being replaced by Photofit, a similar system which used photographs of facial features to construct a composite image of a face. The Bible John investigation was one of the first in the UK to use the new Photofit system when Jeannie Langford was asked to help construct another image of the man that she had seen at the Barrowland Ballroom and in the taxi afterwards.

The use of artists to create an image of a suspect had been in use for much longer – one of the first UK police artist's impressions was released in 1911 during the hunt for Dr Crippen. However, this requires a very particular set of skills – not only must the practitioner be a talented artist, they must also be adept at extracting information from witnesses. This is not a common combination of skills and there is no evidence that during the production of the initial image of Bible John artist Lennox Paterson was allowed to talk to witnesses before creating his painting – it seems that he was simply given witness descriptions and constructed the image from these.

Where does all this leave us in terms of identifying Bible

John? First, we need to consider the various descriptions of Bible John. At the time of the murder of Patricia Docker, there were several witnesses who remembered seeing the nurse dancing with various partners at the Barrowland Ballroom, but these witnesses weren't interviewed until several days later (because of the initial confusion about where Patricia had gone dancing that evening) and none were particularly detailed. No-one remembered seeing her leave, though some of the witnesses thought she might have danced with a tall, red-haired man.

When Mima McDonald was murdered, witnesses saw her drinking at Betty's Bar and dancing at the ballroom with a tall, slim, red-haired, smartly dressed young man. At least two witnesses described the man as very tall – six feet or more, aged twenty-five to thirty five and wearing a dark blue suit with hand-stitched lapels and a white shirt and dark tie. One man and one woman gave a detailed, but still fairly general description of the man's facial features (one saw him in Betty's Bar and the other sitting on a sofa in the Barrowland Ballroom with Mima McDonald). It was these descriptions which were given to George Lennox Paterson who used them to create the first portrait of Bible John.

Jeannie Langford gave police a much more detailed description of the man who had spent the evening with Helen Puttock. This was similar to the description given by the witnesses who had seen the man with Mima McDonald, but it added new details such as the crooked teeth. When Jeannie Langford was taken to Marine police station in Partick for the first time to be interviewed by DS Joe Beattie, she saw the drawing by Lennox Patterson on the wall of his office and immediately said: *'That's him!'* The painting had been released to the press on 26th August 1969 and featured in newspapers and posters and shown on television for two months before the murder of Helen Puttock. Jeannie Langford's description of her reaction to seeing the painting on Joe Beattie's wall implies strongly that she hadn't seen it before and that as soon as she saw it, she recognized it as Helen's killer. She later spent time with George Lennox Paterson who spent time refining the portrait according to her advice. This second version of the portrait was not significantly different to the first. Jeannie Langford then spent time with a Glasgow City Police Photofit technician producing a Photofit of the face of Bible John which also looks very similar to the portrait produced by Lennox Paterson.

Let's just think about all this for a moment. This means that the initial portrait produced by George Lennox Paterson was so accurate that Jeannie Langford recognized it immediately as the man that she saw with her sister in the ballroom. This implies two things: first, that the portrait produced by Lennox Paterson of the murderer of Mima McDonald was very accurate and second, that Mima McDonald and Helen Puttock were murdered by the same man.

Let's first consider the initial portrait produced by Lennox Paterson. This was created when the police sent him descriptions from witnesses who had seen a man with Mima McDonald – there is no record of Lennox Paterson talking with these witnesses, so it appears he created the image purely based on the descriptions they had given the police. In these circumstances, the chances of producing an image that was a close likeness must have been surpassingly small. Yet, when Jeanne saw this portrait in Marine police station, she immediately exclaimed *'That's him!'* She later described how this image was so accurate that it gave her *'a wee kind of shiver of something.'*

The implication is that Jeannie hadn't seen the painting of the killer of Mima McDonald until the day she saw it in Marine police station, but I find this very hard to believe. The murder of Mima McDonald had been widely publicized and the first painting of Bible John had been featured in newspapers and on television. A copy of the painting was even stuck prominently on a notice-board at the Barrowland Ballroom on the night that Helen and Jeannie went there to dance – this was a police poster asking anyone who recognized the man to contact them about the murder of Mima McDonald, and it was displayed in a number of Glasgow dance venues. Before Helen and Jeannie went out that night, their mother Jean had even mentioned the murder of Mima McDonald and suggested that it might be safer if they stayed at home or went somewhere else to dance, though both women ignored her suggestion.

For these reasons, I don't believe that Jeannie Langford saw the painting of Bible John for the first time in the Marine police station, even though that is what her account implies – she simply must have seen it before then. Jeannie heard about the murder of her sister on 31st October, soon after George Puttock, but she was reportedly so distraught that it was only a few days later that she felt able to talk to police. Some accounts claim that it was anything up to two weeks later before police took a detailed statement from Jeannie, though this surely can't be true because Glasgow newspapers on 4th November were already discussing the killer's propensity for quoting the Bible, something that can only have come from Jeannie.

In the period between hearing about her sister's death and talking to the police, I cannot believe that Jeannie hadn't at least considered the possibility that her sister had been killed by the same person who murdered Mima McDonald.

I would also have thought it very likely that she had read newspaper reports about Helen's death which suggested a link between the two murders and carried the original Lennox Paterson portrait of the killer.

These things are important because they suggest at least a possibility that, in Jeannie Langford's memory, the face in the painting by Lennox Paterson had become confused with or had even overlaid the face of the man she saw on the evening of Helen's death. In an article published in Psychology Today in 2016 titled *Revisiting the Places of Memory*, psychologist Robert N. Kraft Ph.D. notes that:

> '*Another notable type of memory error is the conflating of images from different events at the same location. People and events from different times can be combined, like superimposed imagery.*'

It's not uncommon for us to remember a particular person being present during a particular event, even when they weren't – our minds are conflating the memory of a person with a memory of an event to produce an inaccurate composite recollection. I believe that there is at least a possibility that this has happened in the case of Jeannie Langford's memory of the face of the man who killed her sister. I think she was (perhaps unconsciously) already aware of the painting of the face of the man who was the suspect in the Mima McDonald case, and in her mind this may have unwittingly partly overwritten the actual face of the man with whom she shared a taxi.

This would certainly explain what is, for me, a very troubling aspect of this case, and that's the supposed accuracy of the first Lennox Paterson painting. Given how it was created (by the reading of not particularly detailed witness descriptions from the Mima McDonald case), it just can't be an accurate image of the killer's face. Yet Jeannie Langford claimed that she immediately recognised the face and that it was exactly like the man she and her sister had spent the evening with. I think that's because she, (like most people in Glasgow) had already seen this painting and in her memory, this became the face of Bible John.

This would also explain why other witnesses did not agree with Jeannie. The manager of the Barrowland Ballroom, for example, was emphatic that the painting did not in any way resemble the man with who he had argued about the cigarette machine on 30th October 1969. Joe Beattie decided to go with Jeannie Langford's memory and to push Lennox Paterson's painting as an accurate representation of their suspect, but other detectives were very unhappy about this. One, Bryan McLaughlin, even told a Scottish newspaper much later that he had spoken with both the manager and bouncers at the ballroom and they all agreed that the painting was wrong – they were emphatic, for example, that the man was of no more than average height and had much darker, possibly black hair.

As far as most people are concerned, the Lennox Paterson painting has become the face of Bible John. The search for this killer has been predicated on this and various suspects have been accepted or rejected largely on the basis of whether they look like the painting. But, what if this isn't the face of Bible John?

Chapter 12: Will the real Bible John please step forward?

In 1978, West Yorkshire Police were in the midst of their biggest ever investigation – the search for a serial killer who had become known as the Yorkshire Ripper. This was one of the largest investigations ever undertaken by a British police force and in those pre-computer days, information was stored on thousands and thousands of handwritten index cards. The investigation accumulated so much paperwork over the course of an investigation that spanned several years that the floor of the incident room had to be specially reinforced.

Investigators were in danger of being overwhelmed by information when, beginning in March 1978, they received the first of three letters which purported to come from the killer. The first letter was addressed to Assistant Chief Constable George Oldfield, the man leading the Ripper investigation. Over the course of the next twelve months, two more letters were received and in 1979, a cassette tape arrived in the incident room. This contained a message for George Oldfield from the writer of the letters.

After analysing the letters and the tape, West Yorkshire Police concluded that they were genuine and that the distinctive voice on the tape with a Wearside accent was the voice of the Yorkshire Ripper. On 26th June 1979, the tape was released to the media. Police spent around £1 million on a campaign to publicise the taped message in the hope that someone would recognize the voice. They set up a *'Dial-the-Ripper'* telephone hotline, took out full page advertisements in newspapers and put posters on billboards. Around forty thousand men were investigated purely because they came from the Wearside area. Most importantly, suspects who did not have a Wearside accent were virtually disregarded.

In January 1981, a man named Peter Sutcliffe was arrested for driving a car which was displaying stolen number plates. During subsequent interviews, Sutcliffe confessed to being the Yorkshire Ripper. He didn't have a Wearside accent, and as soon as he was arrested it was clear that the tape was a hoax. This had completely derailed the police investigation of these murders for more than two years. Sutcliffe had been interviewed nine times in all during the investigation but, because he didn't have a Wearside accent, he was dismissed as a suspect. Three women were killed by Sutcliffe after the tape was received and before he was caught. The implication is that, if the police had not accepted and publicised the tape as being the voice of the Yorkshire Ripper, Sutcliffe might have been caught sooner and the deaths of some of those women prevented.

Assistant Chief Constable George Oldfield, who had been one of the main supporters of the tape, was disgraced and took early retirement almost as soon as Sutcliffe was arrested.

How is all this relevant to Bible John? Well, accepting the hoax tape as genuine caused the Yorkshire Ripper investigation to head in the wrong direction, leading to West Yorkshire Police investigators ignoring suspects who didn't have a Wearside accent. I suspect that Joe Beattie's acceptance that the Lennox Paterson portrait was an accurate image of Bible John may have derailed the investigation of those murders in precisely the same way. Suspects who didn't have red hair or didn't resemble the portrait were essentially disregarded by police looking for Bible John. If the portrait isn't accurate, this may have caused police to ignore the real killer.

Joe Beattie was aware that not everyone was happy with his complete acceptance of the evidence of Jeannie Langford, though he remained a vociferous supporter of her testimony. He described her as *'a wee sharp Glasgow woman'* and seemed to believe that her description of Bible John was accurate and reliable. He even seemed willing to ignore the fact that Jeannie had a fair amount to drink before going in to the Barrowland Ballroom with Helen that night. The manager told police that she seemed *'drunk'* during the altercation over the cigarette machine. Jeannie claimed that she was no more than '*tipsy*' (slightly drunk) by the time that she got into the taxi with Helen and Bible John. Jeannie certainly admitted to having more than one whisky in the Trader's Tavern before going to the ballroom that night, and we do need to keep this in mind when considering her testimony.

Even Joe Beattie indirectly seemed to suggest that he wasn't quite as sure about her testimony as he sometimes claimed. After his retirement, he mentioned during more than one newspaper interview that he had come to believe that the hunt for Bible John may have been a waste of time because the three murders could have been committed by three different people. However, it was Jeannie Langford's testimony that linked the suspect for the Mima McDonald murder and the suspect for the murder of Helen Puttock. If Jeanie's testimony is reliable, the same man committed both these murders. If two different men committed these murders, as Joe Beattie seemed to come to believe, Jeannie's testimony can't be reliable. If Jeannie Langford's testimony isn't reliable, then the Lennox Paterson portrait may not after all be the face of Bible John.

I strongly suspect that within the files of Glasgow City Police there is a record of an interview with the murderer of Patricia Docker, Mima McDonald and Helen Puttock. I believe that this man was never taken seriously as a suspect because he didn't resemble the Lennox Paterson portrait. Fifty years on, there is no realistic way to re-set this investigation and go back to interview the original suspects. Bible John is now at least in his mid-seventies, if he is still alive. Most witnesses who are still alive are of a similar age and the chances of their recollections still being reliable are essentially zero.

Sadly, I think that a basic mistake in the initial investigation meant that the initial investigation had no chance of identifying the killer. That initial failure means that we will almost certainly never know for certain who Bible John really was.

Chapter 13: Was there really a Bible John?

There are just two more things that we need to consider in our examination of this fascinating case. The first is: Was there really a Bible John at all? Some people think that these three murders were committed by different men and that there never was a single killer. The second thing is that, if the evidence suggests that he did exist, we need to ask why Bible John might have stopped killing?

Let's start by considering whether these murders could have been committed by three different killers. The murders attributed to Bible John are: The murder of Patricia Docker in February 1968, the murder of Mima McDonald in August 1969 and the murder of Helen Puttock in October 1969. Other writers have attempted to link this murderer to additional killings, but none have found any other unsolved murder in the UK in the years following 1969 which share the same MO and signature. I think it is safe to assume that there were just three Bible John Murders.

After his retirement in 1976, Joe Beattie seemed to come to believe that these murders could have been committed by three different people (though he wasn't completely consistent in this). Like some other police officers, he came to think that the story of Bible John was no more than an urban myth created by frenzied newspaper reporting.

This, Beattie claimed, was why it proved impossible to find Bible John. Police were looking for a man who had committed all three murders. If a suspect had an alibi for one or two of the murders, then clearly he couldn't be Bible John and he was eliminated as a suspect. However, if there were really three different murderers, then this approach would have led to eliminating suspects on a false basis.

Is it possible that there really were three different murderers? Looking at the profile of Bible John we developed in Chapter 8, this seems unlikely to me. The MO and signature across all three murders is very similar indeed. There are minor differences between the first murder, that of Patricia Docker, and the other two (Docker's clothes were removed from the scene and there was no evidence that she had been sexually assaulted, for example), but these could be explained by the murderer developing his technique and becoming more confident. The similarities between the murders seem to me to outweigh these minor differences: All three women met their killer at an over-25s night at the Barrowland Ballroom, all three were accompanied by their killer from the ballroom to an isolated location close to their homes, all three were punched and kicked in the head and face before being strangled with a ligature, all three were menstruating at the time of their murders and in all three cases their sanitary pad was placed close to or on the body. Finally, all three victim's handbags were removed from the scene of the murder. To me, these distinct similarities sound very much like the MO and signature of a single killer.

One of the reasons that some police officers have come to the conclusion that there must have been separate killers seems to be a feeling that, if one man had really committed all three murders and the Lennox Paterson portrait was a good likeness, then they surely would have caught him? However, if the portrait wasn't a good likeness, this would also explain why they failed to find their man, even if a single killer was involved.

There was another reason that caused police to wonder whether this might not have been the work of one man. Bible John seems to have stopped killing after the murder of Helen Puttock (or at least, no-one has been able to identify any other plausible victims). Sexual serial killers were a relatively new phenomenon in the late 1960s and the general view by psychologists at the time was that these people ware helplessly impelled to kill by overpowering and uncontrollable urges. Once they started killing, they not only couldn't stop, the period between killings would inevitably reduce as the killer sought to reproduce the elation of the first murder. Dr. Scott Bonn, criminologist and author of the book '*Why We Love Serial Killers: The Curious Appeal of the World's Most Savage Murderers*', sums up this view of these killers:

> '*Serial killing is almost like a drug addiction. It's a compulsion. They have to have it and they do it again and again until they are caught or killed.*'

This view of serial murderers suggests that if a series of killings committed by sexual serial killer should suddenly stop, that could only be because the killer has died, or become seriously ill, or been imprisoned or has moved to another part of the country (where the killings will, of course, continue).

Based on this prevailing psychological view of a serial killer, police looking for Bible John began to look for explanations for why the killings appeared to stop after the murder of Helen Puttock. They looked at men from Glasgow of the right age range who had died or been sent to prison and at members of the armed forces who had been posted away from the UK at the relevant time. They found no viable suspects in this way despite exhaustive investigations. Therefore, the thinking went, if sexual serial killers can't stop, but there were only these three murders, well, then perhaps these killings were the work of three separate killers, each succumbing to a sudden but singular murderous impulse after spending the evening at the

Barrowland Ballroom.

We now know that this notion is based on a fallacious view of the psychology of sexual serial killer. The availability of more data relating to this type of killer has led to a new view of their behaviour and it's now believed that the idea that sexual serials can't stop killing is completely mistaken. Horribly, for some of these killers murder seems to be akin to a hobby – something to be enjoyed when time and circumstances permit and to be held in abeyance when they don't. These people aren't generally the helpless victims of their own urges that psychologists would have had us believe in the past – they are people who choose to satisfy these urges when they can do so with the least chance of being caught.

Take, for example, the American rapist and murderer who became known as the Golden State Killer. Between April 1974 and July 1981, this person committed at least twelve murders, more than fifty rapes and hundreds of burglaries in California. Then, he seemed to stop killing, raping and committing burglaries for five years until his final murder in April 1986. All these crimes remained unsolved but police and criminologists searching for the Golden State Killer compiled a profile in the 1980s which confidently noted that this person *would continue committing violent crimes until incapacitated by prison, death, or other intervention.*' But, there was a gap of over five years between his second last and last murders and after May 1986, the murders, rapes and burglaries stopped. Completely.

For the next thirty years, people speculated about the identity of this killer and about what could have happened to prompt the long gaps between the last killings and to eventually stop this prolific sexual serial killer and rapist. Had he been sent to prison for some unrelated offence? Had he died? Had he moved elsewhere in the US? Did he have a job that required him to leave the country? Had he changed his MO to the extent that his killings were no longer recognized as belonging to the series?

Then, in April 2018, police arrested ex-police officer James DeAngelo in connection with these crimes. Seventy-four year old DeAngelo had been identified almost by chance when DNA from a family member was found to be a close match for DNA taken from Golden State Killer crime scenes. A test of DNA from DeAngelo proved beyond doubt that he is the Golden State Killer.

But, why did he stop killing in 1981 for five years and then stop completely in 1986? DeAngelo hasn't spoken, so all we can do is speculate. During the second to last murder committed in 1981, DeAngelo was involved in a violent confrontation with the victim's boyfriend and he was

113

injured. Perhaps this frightened him so much that he stopped for five years? Police investigators have also wondered if DeAngelo, who was thirty-five in 1981, may have come to find the physical effort of committing these crimes too much as he grew older?

I would suggest that there is another, simpler, explanation. In 1981, DeAngelo's wife gave birth to a daughter, the couple's first child. DeAngelo wouldn't be the first man to find that his life was completely changed by a new child and that time for previously precious hobbies was severely curtailed. I believe that DeAngelo may have stopped killing and raping simply because he no longer had the leisure time required to do these things. It's also worth noting that the final murder in 1986 took place at around the time that DeAngelo's wife was giving birth to their second child. Perhaps he took advantage of his wife's absence in hospital to commit one final murder?

By coincidence, and just before DeAngelo was arrested, in March 2018 the FBI Behavioural Analysis Unit published a report, 'Serial Murder - Multi-Disciplinary Perspectives for Investigators' which provided information for law enforcement personnel on common misconceptions about serial killers. This noted, amongst other things, that some serial killers do suddenly stop committing their crimes and highlighted two examples which confirm this: Dennis

Rader, also known as the BTK killer, who murdered ten people between 1974 and 1991 and then stopped killing and Jeffrey Gorton who killed his first victim in 1986, his second in 1991 and his third and final victim in 2002. The report concluded that: *'circumstances can change in a serial killer's life causing them to stop killing before they are caught. These could include increased participation in family activities, sexual substitution, and other diversions.'*

When James DeAngelo was arrested just a few weeks after the publication of this report, what was known about his crimes backed-up this assertion. DeAngelo did stop killing, but not because he was dead, incapacitated or incarcerated.

In the light of this new information about the psychology of serial killers, I think the notion that Bible John would not (or could not) stop killing is mistaken. I believe that the murders of Patricia Docker, Mima McDonald and Helen Puttock were committed by the same man and that he stopped killing after the last murder. He may have become frightened by the massive police and media interest after the third murder and made a conscious decision to stop killing. He may have got married, become a father or undergone some other change in his personal or professional circumstances which reduced his need to stalk and kill women or made it more difficult for him to safely do so.

Overall, I believe that an analysis of the evidence and the circumstances of these murders strongly suggest that there really was a single killer who committed three murders in Glasgow in the late 1960s. I also believe that what we now know about the psychology of serial killers means that it is entirely possible that he may have decided to stop killing after his third murder for reasons we don't fully understand.

Chapter 14: Putting it all together

Over the previous thirteen chapters, we have looked at everything that it known about Bible John. Now, it's time to put all this together and see where that leaves us.

What we know about this killer makes it seem almost certain that he was raised in the Glasgow area and had a Glasgow accent. He had crooked front teeth and a missing tooth on his upper right jaw. His neat appearance suggests that he had a white-collar job of some sort and that he was used to giving instructions and having these followed. He was articulate and capable of charm when required. He was of above average height and slim and there seems to be a consensus amongst witnesses that he was between twenty-five and thirty-five years of age. He appeared to be comfortable within the milieu of the Barrowland Ballroom, but he seems not to have been a regular attendee there. He may have had some knowledge of police investigative procedure. The anger displayed by this killer may have been at least partly prompted by the fact that each of his victims was menstruating.

This is a frighteningly short list of reasonable assertions we can make about Bible John, especially when weighed against the fallacies associated with this killer.

For example, the notion that he was obsessed by the Bible

and/or very religious appears to be based on hyperbolic newspaper reporting rather than hard evidence. The only person who mentioned a possible link with the Bible was Jeannie Langford, and she only mentioned his possibly quoting from the Bible once. Both she and Joe Beattie had concerns about both the newspaper reporting and the name this killer was commonly given because these seemed to imply a much greater interest in the Bible than the suspect actually demonstrated.

As noted earlier in this book, I believe that the single greatest fallacy associated with this murderer was an assumption that we know what he looked like. I have grave doubts that Bible John looked like the painting by George Lennox Paterson and I believe that this assumption badly hampered the police investigation and most subsequent attempts to identify this killer. Even the often quoted '*facts*' that he was notably tall and had red hair were not things that all witnesses were agreed upon.

For the reasons explained earlier, I don't believe that any of the people who have been named as potential suspects in this case are Bible John. I wish that I could end this book by highlighting a particular suspect that I believe to be Bible John but I cannot honestly do that without risking adding yet another layer of fallacy to a case that is already mired in misconception and outright falsehood.

If there is to be a genuine attempt to identify this killer, then it can only come through starting again and re-examining suspects on the basis of what is actually known about this killer and ignoring those pieces of evidence that are mistaken or doubtful. I'm not certain that, after the passage of fifty years this is even possible, but another book identifying someone on the basis that they *'look like Bible John'* is not what is needed (you will have noted that almost all the people named in the *'Suspects'* part of this book have been suggested because they supposedly resemble the painting of Bible John).

The deterioration of the DNA evidence taken from Helen Puttock's body means that this type of analysis can't be used to definitively identify or exclude any potential suspect, so finding this killer could only be done by old-fashioned detective work and deductive reasoning. With the passage of more than fifty years, I don't believe that this is possible.

Conclusion

George Lennox Paterson was an artist of real talent. His painting of Bible John isn't just a likeness, it's a portrait of a man wearing a cold, supercilious and rather aloof expression. It is in fact just how most of us would imagine a religiously inclined sexual serial killer to look. It's a great painting and I believe it may have been a major factor in preventing the identification of the murderer of Patricia Docker, Mima McDonald and Helen Puttock.

For the reasons explained in this book, I believe that the circumstances in which the first version of this painting was produced make it surpassingly unlikely that it is a good likeness of the man who walked Mima McDonald home from the Barrowland Ballroom in August 1969. I think that Jeannie Langford was aware of this painting before her sister's murder and in her memory, this face became conflated and confused with the face of the man she met at the Barrowland Ballroom in October 1969. Human memory is a fallible and malleable thing and in this case, failures in accurate recall may have allowed this killer to escape justice.

I think this contention is supported by several witnesses who claimed that the portrait bore no resemblance to the man they had seen that evening in the ballroom. Mainly on the instructions of Joe Beattie, it was the recollection of Jeannie Langford that was given precedence over all others. But even the Photofit which Jeannie Langford worked with police to produce has one important difference – it clearly shows a man with much darker hair than the Lennox Paterson painting (and that agrees with what some other witnesses reported), yet there was at the time and remains a common belief that Bible John had red or sandy hair.

Just like the Yorkshire Ripper investigation ten years later, I believe that the Bible John investigation was hamstrung by emphasis on a piece of evidence which may be mistaken. In the case of the Yorkshire Ripper investigation, police weren't convinced the tape was a hoax until they caught Peter Sutcliffe, the real killer. Bible John was never caught but if he had been, I strongly suspect that whatever he looked like, it wouldn't have been anything like the painting by Lennox Paterson.

I think the evidence suggests that this murderer was real and he took the lives of three innocent women, but I think that almost every significant aspect of what is commonly thought to be known about Bible John is mistaken. I think that his real face is still a mystery, I don't believe that he was particularly interested in the Bible and I very much doubt that his name was John. Take these things away and we are left with a faceless killer about who we really know very little. This man may still be living quietly in Scotland or elsewhere, perhaps smiling wryly if ever he happens to see a print of that famous painting. You may have met him. You may know him. You may live next door to him. But you will never know because so much that has been said and written about this case is simply wrong.

Bible John became famous at least partly because of the catchy name given to him by newspapers and by George Lennox Paterson's painting. But I believe that these things also served to obscure his real identity and ensure that the real face of Bible John is as unknown to us now as it was in 1969.

I hope you enjoyed reading this book. If you did, please take a moment to leave me a review on Amazon. Your opinion matters and positive reviews help me greatly. Thank you.

I also welcome feedback from readers. If you have comments on this book or ideas for other books in the Murder World series, please send me an email at: stevemac357@gmail.com.

Bibliography

Non-Fiction

Bible John: Search for a Sadist, by Charles Stoddart, 1980. It's not easy to find a copy of this book now, but solicitor Charles Stoddart produced this factual and unsensational book about the Bible John case which includes a detailed look at the murders and the subsequent police investigation.

Glasgow Crimefighter: The Les Brown Story, by Les brown and Robert Jeffrey, 2005. Les Brown was a police detective working in Glasgow during the Bible John Murders. In Chapter 6 of this autobiography he puts forward his idea that a Glasgow man named John Edgar was Bible John.

Glasgow's Hard Men: True Crime from the Files of The Herald, Evening Times and Sunday Herald, by Robert Jeffrey, 2006. This book is a discussion of crime in Glasgow in the 1950s, 60s and 70s, mainly drawn from contemporary newspaper reports. Chapter 9, *The face a city can never forget*, is concerned with Bible John and provides interesting background information.

Bible John's Secret Daughter: Murder, Drugs and a Mother's Secret Heartbreak, by David Leslie, 2007. A book in which a young woman claims that her mother was raped by Bible John after she had spent the evening at the Barrowland Ballroom in the late 1960s and that she may therefore be his daughter. The author presents nothing in the way of evidence to back up the claim that the woman, Hannah Martin, was actually attacked by this killer other than her assertion that the man who raped her was said to have looked like the portrait of Bible John. This book doesn't really add anything to knowledge of the Bible John case.

The Lost British Serial Killer, by David Wilson and Paul Harrison, 2010. This book makes a case that convicted serial killer Peter Tobin was Bible John. However, there are doubts that Tobin could have been the killer of Mima McDonald (because he was in Brighton with his first wife at the time that this murder took place) and reasons to doubt that he killed Helen Puttock (he is for example, much shorter than most eyewitness descriptions of Bible John). Still a well-written book which provides a great deal of background to this case.

Dancing with the Devil: The Bible John Murders, by Paul Harrison, 2013. Harrison is an ex-police officer who has published a number of true-crime books including co—authoring a book with David Wilson which claimed that Peter Tobin was Bible John. In this one he claims that he has identified Bible John and that he is a retired police officer who can't be named for legal reasons. He bases this on conversations he had with Joe Beattie, the officer in charge of the Bible John investigation.

Television

BBC Documentary. In September 1970 the British Broadcasting Company broadcast a thirty minute documentary on the Bible John murders hosted by presenter Hugh Cochrane. This summarised the murders and the (lack of) progress in the Glasgow City Police investigation and concluded with an appeal for the killer to give himself up.

Unsolved: Getting Away with Murder – Bible John was a documentary on the Bible John murders which was part of the '*Unsolved*' documentary series produced by Grampian Television (now STV North) and first broadcast in December 2005. This focused on the murder of Helen Puttock and speculated that Peter Tobin might have been her murderer. The show appealed for viewers to call in if they had additional information on the crimes features, but the Bible John episode doesn't seem to have generated any new leads.

In Search of Bible John was a forty-five minute documentary broadcast by STV in 2011 which mainly looked at the possibility that Peter Tobin was Bible John.

Bible John in Fiction

Black and Blue, 1997, by Ian Rankin. The eighth in the popular Inspector Rebus series of crime novels sees Rebus investigate (amongst other things) the Bible John murders. He identifies a prime suspect, but the man kills a murderer that Rebus is pursuing and vanishes before Rebus can confront him. This was also the first of the Rebus novels to be adapted for television , starring John Hannah as Inspector Rebus and being first shown in 2000 as *Rebus*.

The Quaker, 2018, by Liam McIlvanney. Set in Glasgow in 1969, this novel follows Detective Inspector McCormack as he searches for Bible John. Great sense of place and time and a pretty good crime story too – this book won the Scottish Crime Fiction award for 2018.

About the Author

Steve MacGregor is a Scot who writes non-fiction on a range of topics including true crime and the paranormal. He has been interested in crime writing since he read his first true crime book at the local library in 1971, when everyone thought he was studying for his homework. Now he doesn't have to do it in secret anymore and reads a range of work by various crime writers.

He is married with two grown-up children and currently lives in Andalucía in Spain.

Other Murder World Scotland books

If you enjoyed this book, you may also be interested in these other Murder World Scotland Books which are also available on Amazon:

Death in a cold town: The Arlene Fraser case

One Morning in April 1998, attractive mother and housewife Arlene Fraser called her children's school in the town of Elgin on the Moray coast of Scotland. She wanted to know what time her son would be returning from a school trip? That was the last time that anyone had contact with Arlene. When a friend arrived at her house two hours later, she found no sign of Arlene and no-one has seen her since.

The search for Arlene Fraser became one of the biggest and longest running missing person cases ever seen in Scotland but no clue was found to indicate what had happened to her. Was she abducted and murdered on the instructions of Nat, her estranged husband as the police claimed? Did she run away to a new life, leaving her children, her home and her friends behind? Was she somehow involved in smuggling?

This book provides a detailed look at Arlene Fraser's disappearance, the trials and the legal manoeuvring and appeals which followed. It also analyses the main theories of what may have happened to Arlene to assess which is the most likely.

A killing at kinky cottage: The murder of Max Garvie

The Swinging sixties eventually reached even the tranquil Howe O' the Mearns in the North-East of Scotland. Millionaire farmer Max Garvie and his glamorous wife Sheila became so well-known for their nudist and sex parties that their farmhouse became known locally as '*kinky cottage.*'

However, beneath the swinging exterior, all was not well in the marriage of Max and Sheila. Max was easily bored and constantly sought new sexual adventures and partners. Sheila was interested in a more stable and lasting relationship, but not with Max.

Then, one evening in May 1968, the peace and quiet of this tranquil farming community was ripped apart by a shotgun blast. It seemed that Sheila had finally found a permanent way to solve her marital problems. But was it really that simple?

The Butler's Story: The extraordinary life and crimes of Archibald Thomson Hall

Archibald Thompson Hall was a complicated man. A bisexual born in the working-class back streets of Glasgow, he craved culture and the finer things in life. Sadly, his life hadn't equipped him with the means to obtain these so he stole them instead. He worked as a burglar, thief and con-man for many years before stumbling on a role that suited him well – he became a butler and transformed himself into the urbane, charming and imperturbable gentleman's gentleman Roy Fontaine.

Working as a butler certainly gave him opportunities to steal and embezzle from his employers, but it also led him to face arrest, conviction and prison on more than one occasion (though he became the first person to escape from one of Britain's first high-security prisons). It wasn't until 1977, when he was fifty-three, that he finally discovered his true vocation as a murderer. He committed his first murder in November 1977 and by January the following year he had killed five people and would almost certainly have gone on to kill many more if he hadn't been caught.

This is the true story of a charming, charismatic, intelligent, entertaining, cold, ruthless and merciless killer and one of the most dangerous men in the annals of Scottish crime.

The Vanishing: The Renee MacRae case

One November evening in 1976, Renee MacRae, the estranged wife of a millionaire Scottish businessman, set off from her luxury home in Inverness. She was going, she had told her husband, to spend the weekend with her sister in Kilmarnock and she took her three year old son Andrew with her.

Four hours later her BMW car was found burning in a remote lay-by on the A9, the main road to the south from Inverness. In the car there was no sign of Renee, Andrew or their luggage.

Police enquiries quickly discovered that Renee's real reason for leaving Inverness was very different to the story she had told her estranged husband and discovered that her life was rather more complicated than it appeared from the outside. The search for the missing mother and son was huge and this became the longest running missing person investigation in Scottish history. Despite this, no trace of Renee or Andrew was ever found.

Officially, Renee MacRae is still missing and no-one has

ever been charged with her murder or that of her son. However, over the forty years that have passed since she vanished, tantalizing clues have emerged that allow us to consider the various theories, to work out the most likely course of events that November night and to identify the person most likely to have caused the disappearance.

37678772R00079

Printed in Great Britain
by Amazon